FOCUS ON
Comprehension

Teacher's Resource
for Books 3 and 4

Nelson Thornes

First published in 1999 by:
Thomas Nelson & Sons Ltd

Reprinted in 2002 by:
Nelson Thornes Ltd
Delta Place
27 Bath Road
CHELTENHAM
GL53 7TH
United Kingdom

08 09 / 10

A catalogue record of this book is available from the British Library

ISBN 978 0 17 420297 4

Cover illustrations by Jill Newton
Illustrations by Peter Bailey, Carla Daly, Phil Garner, Janet Simmonett,
Kate Sheppard and Gary Taylor
Page make-up by Susan Clarke

Printed and bound in Croatia by Zrinski

Acknowledgments
The author and publishers wish to thank the following for permission to produce
copyright materials, as follows:

Hodder and Stoughton for the poem, *A Ghostly ABC from Wordgames* by Sandy
Brownjohn; Walker Books Ltd., London for *Why Do Dogs Chase Cars?* from South
and North, East and West, edited text © 1992 Michael Rosen; Anita Marie Sackett
for the poem *Grandma* published by Scholastic Ltd.; The Literary Trustees of Walter
de la Mare, and the Society of Authors as their representative, for *The Listeners by*
Walter de la Mare; The James Reeves Estate for *The Osc* © James Reeves from the
Complete Poems for Children (Heinemann); Richard Edwards for *A Mouse in My
Roof*, first published in the UK by Orchard Books (Watts Publishing Group) 1988.

Please note: we have tried to trace and contact all copyright holders before
publication, but this has not always been possible. If notified, we, the publishers, will
be pleased to make any amendments or arrangements at the first opportunity.

CONTENTS

WHAT IS COMPREHENSION?

The *Concise Oxford Dictionary* defines comprehension as 'the act or capability of understanding, especially writing or speech'. In the context of school, the ability to gain meaning from the printed word is of paramount importance.

A helpful way of looking at comprehension is to treat it as a range of skills. Thomas Barrett, quoted in *Reading Today and Tomorrow*[1], suggests a taxonomy of comprehension skills. This provides a very useful model, and was used as a framework for developing and structuring the *Focus on Comprehension* series.

Barrett divides reading comprehension into five major skill levels which move from the easy to the difficult in terms of the demands they place on the reader. The categories he suggests are:

▶ Literal Comprehension
  This focuses on ideas and information explicitly stated in the text. The tasks may involve recognition or recall of details, main ideas, sequences, cause and effect, character traits and so on.

▶ Reorganisation
  This requires the child to analyse and/or reorganise ideas or information explicitly stated in the text. For example, tasks may involve classifying, outlining or summarising.

▶ Inferential Comprehension
  This requires the child to use information and ideas explicitly stated in the text, along with intuition and personal experiences as a basis for making deductions and hypotheses. The child is required to use thinking and imagination that go beyond the printed page.

▶ Evaluation
  This requires the reader to evaluate a text, by comparing ideas presented with external criteria (such as other similar sources), or internal criteria (such as by drawing on the reader's own experiences, knowledge or values). Evaluative comprehension deals with qualities of accuracy, acceptability, desirability, worth or probability of occurrence.

▶ Appreciation
  This involves the subjective response of the impact of the text on the reader. It requires some sort of emotional response to the content, characters or incidents, author's use of language or imagery.

In summary, categories of Barrett's taxonomy of comprehension skills are as follows:
▶ read the lines (using literal comprehension)
▶ read between the lines (using reorganisation and inference)
▶ read beyond the lines (using evaluative and appreciative comprehension).

Focus on Comprehension used this three-fold classification to develop three categories of differentiated activities, designed to help children develop a wide range of comprehension skills.

[1] T. Barrett, quoted in Theodore Clymer, 'What is reading? Some current concepts', Open University 1968 in *Reading Today and Tomorrow*, University of London Press 1972.

STATUTORY AND NON-STATUTORY GUIDANCE

The teaching of reading is a statutory requirement in the UK. *Focus on Comprehension* has been developed against the backcloth of the statutory requirements of England and Wales, Scotland and Northern Ireland and the objectives of the National Literacy Project.

The National Curriculum for England and Wales

The National Curriculum expects that pupils' reading will be developed through the use of progressively more challenging and demanding tasks.

The General Requirements of the National Curriculum state that in order to develop as effective readers, pupils should be taught to:
► read accurately, fluently and with understanding
► understand and respond to the texts they read
► read, analyse and evaluate a wide range of texts, including literature from the English literary heritage and from other cultures and traditions.

Key skills, which are identified as important in the Programme of Study at Key Stage 2, are developed in *Focus on Comprehension*, as follows:
► Pupils should be taught to consider in detail the quality and depth of what they read.
► They should be encouraged to respond imaginatively to the plot, characters, ideas, vocabulary and organisation of language in literature.
► They should be taught to use inference and deduction.
► Pupils should be taught to evaluate texts they read, and to refer to relevant passages or episodes to support their opinions.
► Pupils should be taught how to find information in books ... by using organisational devices.
► They should be given opportunities to read for different purposes, adopting appropriate strategies for the task.
► Pupils should be taught to distinguish between fact and opinion ... to consider an argument critically ... to make succinct notes ... to re-present information in different forms ... to note the meaning of newly encountered words ... to use indexes.
► Pupils should be introduced to the organisational, structural and presentational features of different types of text, and to some appropriate terms, to enable them to discuss the texts they read, such as 'author', 'setting'.

Scottish 5-14 Guidelines

The Scottish 5-14 Guidelines include the following in their guidance to teachers:
► Learning to read accurately and with discrimination becomes increasingly important as pupils move through their education.
► The importance of meaning should be stressed at all stages.
► Reading should always have a purpose which is clear. Pupils must ... learn to recognise the more common genres of fiction and non-fiction.
► The teacher needs to deploy a widening range of techniques such as sequencing, prediction, cloze procedure, evaluating the text, making deductions, comparing and contrasting different texts.
► Reading activities should demand that pupils show an overall grasp of a text, an understanding of specific details and how they contribute to the whole, make inferences, supply supporting evidence, and identify intended audience, purpose and features of style.
► Teaching strategies ... will help them to make sense of aspects such as plot, characters and themes.
► The teacher can focus on texts:
  – by directing (pupils) into the task,
  – by providing questions which ask for literal, inferential and evaluative responses,
  – by asking them (pupils) to demonstrate understanding,
  – by asking readers to use the text as a model for their own writing.

Northern Ireland Curriculum

Focus on Comprehension follows the guidance to teachers addressed in The Northern Ireland Curriculum as shown below.

Pupils should have opportunities to:
► read ... from an increasingly wide selection of books;
► discuss their comprehension and interpretation of the texts they have read, justifying their responses logically by inference, deduction and reference to evidence within the text;

Northern Ireland Curriculum continued

- learn that different reading purposes require different reading skills;
- acquire the use of skills necessary to locate information within texts;
- (use resources) making use of organisational devices to locate, select, evaluate and communicate information;
- discuss and consider aspects of stories, for example, characters, places, objects and events, paying attention to what is written and how it is expressed;
- discuss texts, exploring ways in which word meanings can be manipulated;
- reconsider their initial response to texts in the light of insight and information which subsequently emerge in their reading;
- encounter a wide variety of texts;
- respond with sensitivity to what they read, developing the ability to place themselves in someone else's position and extending their capacity for sympathy and empathy;
- speculate on situations read about, predict what may happen or consider what might have happened;
- discuss features of language.

The National Literacy Strategy

As well as taking into account the various UK statutory curriculum requirements, *Focus on Comprehension* has been designed to help schools meet the text level objectives of the National Literacy Strategy. *Focus on Comprehension* follows closely the range of texts and objectives for each year specified by the National Literacy Strategy.

The National Literacy Strategy characterises the literary primary-school pupil as one who is able to:

- read ... with confidence, fluency and understanding;
- orchestrate a full range of reading cues ... monitor their reading and correct their mistakes;
- have an interest in words and their meanings and a growing vocabulary;
- ... understand and be familiar with some of the ways in which narratives are structured through basic literary ideas of setting, character and plot;
- understand and use ... a wide range of non-fiction texts;
- have a suitable technical vocabulary through which to understand and discuss their reading;
- be interested in books, read with enjoyment and evaluate and justify their preferences;
- through reading ... develop their powers of imagination, inventiveness and critical awareness.

COMPONENTS OF
FOCUS ON COMPREHENSION

Year Group	Course Book	Teacher's Resource Book
1	Starter Book (24 pp)	Book 'A' (152 pp) for Starter and Introductory Books
2	Introductory Book (48 pp)	
3	Book 1 (48 pp)	Book 'B' (104 pp) for Books 1 and 2
4	Book 2 (48 pp)	
5	Book 3 (64 pp)	Book 'C' (104 pp) for Books 3 and 4
6	Book 4 (64 pp)	

Pupils' Books – structure and features

▶ Each book is divided into 22 Teaching Units (single A4 pages of stimulus illustrations in the Starter Book; double-pages in Introductory Book and Pupils' Books 1 and 2; two-, three- and four-page units in Pupils' Books 3 and 4)

▶ Each Teaching Unit is structured in the same way, in the Introductory Book through to Book 4, in order to facilitate planning, provide differentiation, make pages easily accessible to pupils.

▶ Five sections appear in each unit, as follows:

Think ahead
- introduces the stimulus reading passage
- poses open-ended questions for whole-class discussion
- provides a clear purpose for reading the passage.

The stimulus passage
- provides the main text to work on
- provides a wide range of fiction and non-fiction texts
- provides progressively more challenging and demanding extracts
- may be used for 'shared' or 'guided' reading.

Thinking back
- provides activities which encourage 'reading the lines', focusing mainly on literal comprehension
- provides suitable activities for a whole class.

Thinking about it
- provides activities at an intermediate level
- encourages 'reading between the lines', focusing mainly on reorganisation and inferential comprehension
- provides activities appropriate for whole class, group or individual work.

Thinking it through
- provides activities at a third, and higher level of differentiation
- encourages 'reading beyond the lines', focusing on evaluative and appreciative comprehension
- provides activities most appropriate for group and individual work.

Teacher's Book – structure and features

The Teacher's Book:

- defines comprehension
- provides information on the aims, approach, and structure of the course
- sets *Focus on Comprehension* in the context of statutory curriculum guidance
- sets *Focus on Comprehension* in the context of the National Literacy Strategy
- provides practical advice on organising and using *Focus on Comprehension* with special reference to the Literacy Hour
- provides detailed answers to each unit
- provides a comprehensive range of further teaching ideas on how to use each unit for further text level activities (in comprehension and writing composition), sentence level and word level work
- includes an accompanying photocopiable activity for each unit
- provides class and individual record sheets and practical assessment suggestions.

Teacher's Book – Copymasters

▶ Each unit has an accompanying copymaster. These copymasters:
- develop or extend the theme or type of activity in the main unit in the pupils' book
- provide a range of activities which may not be appropriate in a textbook format
- provide extracts for comparison or poems/passages by the same author/poet
- provide playlets or poems for performance.

▶ The copymasters may be used alongside the main unit or independently.

▶ They may be used for whole class, group or individual work.

▶ They may be used for homework assignments.

Note: the Starter Book is structured differently from the other pupils' books. This structuring is explained in Teacher's Book 'A'.

OVERVIEW OF RANGE OF TEXTS

Starter Book

Fiction and poetry
Stories with familiar settings; stories, rhymes and poems with familiar, predictable and repetitive patterns, and structures for our culture and other cultures; traditional stories and rhymes; fairy stories; stories based on fantasy worlds; poems with similar themes; plays.

Non-fiction
Signs; labels; captions; lists; instructions; information books and texts; simple dictionaries.

Introductory Book

Fiction and poetry
Stories and poems with familiar settings; traditional stories; stories and poems from other cultures; stories and poems with predictable and patterned language; poems and stories by significant children's poets and authors; texts with language play.

Non-fiction
Instructions; alphabetically ordered texts; explanations; information books including non-chronological reports.

Book 1

Fiction and poetry
Stories with familiar settings; plays; myths, legends, fables; traditional stories; adventure and mystery stories; poems based on observation and the senses; shape poems; oral and performance poetry; humorous poems; poetry with language play.

Non-fiction
Information books; non-chronological reports; thesaurus/dictionary; instructions; letters.

Book 2

Fiction and poetry
Historical texts and poems; plays; imagined works; sci-fi/fantasy; dilemmas and issues; stories and poems from other cultures; classic poetry; modern poetry; range of poetic forms.

Non-fiction
Newspaper/magazine reports; instructions; information texts; explanations; persuasive writing; discussion texts.

Book 3

Fiction and poetry
Stories by significant children's authors; traditional stories (including traditional stories) and poems from other cultures; plays; concrete poetry; classic poetry; narrative poetry; choral and performance poetry.

Non-fiction
Recounts; observational records and reports; instructional texts; explanations; persuasive writing.

Book 4

Fiction and poetry
Classic fiction, poetry and drama; TV/film adaptations; range of genres; range of poetry.

Non-fiction
Autobiography/biography; journalistic writing; reports; discussion texts; formal writing; explanations; reference texts.

Scope and range of individual books

The range of texts is summarised at the front of each of the pupils' books in the form of a scope and sequence chart. This shows the range of texts covered within the fiction and non-fiction categories.

USING *FOCUS ON COMPREHENSION* IN THE CLASSROOM

Focus on Comprehension and the Literacy Hour

Focus on Comprehension has been designed with the National Literacy Project very much in mind. Because it follows closely the range of texts and objectives for each year specified in the framework document, it has great potential for supporting schools teaching the daily Literacy Hour.

Class work

The National Literacy Strategy defines 'shared' reading as a class activity using a common text, such as a text extract in which the teacher reads to and with the class, modelling and discussing texts. *Focus on Comprehension* provides a range of progressively more challenging and demanding extracts and differentiated comprehension questions.

The extract could be shared with the class and discussed, using some of the activities in the pupils' books for discussion or written comprehension responses. (The 'further teaching opportunities' section in the Teacher's Book provides additional suggestions for comprehension work.)

The use of the passage may be extended further to provide related writing composition activities, and classwork arising from the texts at sentence and word level. The 'Further Teaching Opportunities' section of each unit's lesson notes provides for this.

Group work

'Guided' reading is when the teacher focuses on independent reading. The framework document suggests that it should be 'a carefully structured group activity, involving time for sustained reading. Pupils should have individual copies of the same text. The texts need to be carefully selected to match the reading levels of the group.' The structure of the *Focus on Comprehension* books make them ideal for this purpose. The differentiated comprehension activities provide 'questions to direct or check up on the reading, points to note, problems to solve', and so on, which meet the text level objectives in the framework. The teacher could introduce the text to the group (to familiarise them with overall context, and to point out key words) as appropriate, use the differentiated activities to assess the development of comprehension and offer support to each pupil as required. The copymaster for each unit provides further opportunities for this too.

Independent work

Irrespective of whether *Focus on Comprehension* is used for shared and/or guided reading, it also offers enormous potential for additional independent work. The framework document suggests that 'independent tasks could cover a wide range of objectives including comprehension work, independent writing, vocabulary extension and dictionary work, practice and investigations in grammar, punctuation and sentence construction, phonic and spelling investigations and practice'. Children may be asked to complete some of the activity sections following each unit or the related copymasters at this time for additional comprehension work. The 'Further Teaching Opportunities' section of each unit's lesson notes provides numerous ideas for capitalising on the extract in each unit at text, sentence and word level for independent work.

Assessment and record-keeping

A systematic use of the *Focus on Comprehension* course will help children prepare for the statutory and non-statutory assessment requirements.

The tightly-structured nature of the reading material and the differentiated range of comprehension activities help make the ongoing assessment of the children's reading and comprehension skills easy to monitor. It may be considered desirable to ask children to complete one of the units each term (and/or one of the accompanying copymasters) on separate sheets of paper, to keep in their individual portfolios as markers and records of progress and achievement.

Recording pupils' progress is an important aspect of classroom management and good educational practice. Two record sheets are provided. The Class Record Sheet (see page 10) enables you to maintain an overview on class progress as a whole, whereas the Individual Record Sheet (on page 11) enables you to monitor individual progress and achievement.

CLASS RECORD SHEET

Book _____   **Class** _____

Name	Units																					
	1	2	3	4	5	6	7	8	9	10	11	12	13	14	15	16	17	18	19	20	21	22

Note: It is suggested that a pupil's progress for each unit is indicated as follows:

/ = attempted;   × = completed satisfactorily

Focus on Comprehension Teacher's Book 'C'   Text © Louis Fidge 1999 Illustrations © Nelson 1999   Published by Thomas Nelson and Sons Ltd

INDIVIDUAL RECORD SHEET

Name _____ **Book** _____ **Class** _____

Unit	Comment	Date
1		
2		
3		
4		
5		
6		
7		
8		
9		
10		
11		
12		
13		
14		
15		
16		
17		
18		
19		
20		
21		
22		

Focus on Comprehension Teacher's Book 'C'   Text © Louis Fidge 1999 Illustrations © Nelson 1999   Published by Thomas Nelson and Sons Ltd

FURTHER TEACHING OPPORTUNITIES

Text level

Reading comprehension
▶ Encourage the children to compare and contrast the two different types of text, suggesting similarities and differences, and commenting on their different features, their purpose and effectiveness.

Writing composition
▶ Ask children to write a poem, or draw a diagram, showing the cycle of the seasons of the year and what happens in each. The poem or diagram should be set out in a circular form.

Sentence level

Grammatical awareness
▶ Use the sentences in the diagram to investigate word order, by examining how far the order of the words in the sentences can be changed. Which words are essential to meaning? Which can be deleted without affecting the meaning? Which words, or groups of words, can be moved into a different order?

Sentence construction and punctuation
▶ Identify all the verbs in the texts. Discuss the function they serve. A feature of most explanatory texts is that the verbs are in the present tense. Do these texts follow this pattern? Try converting them into the past tense. What changes are needed? Notice, too, that the texts are written in the third person.

Word level

Spelling
▶ Do some work on pluralisation of nouns. Explore and develop rules to cover different situations. Find examples in the text of regular nouns that take 's' in the plural, such as hill, ray. Pluralise these. Ask children to think of words that end in 'sh', 'ch', 'x', 'ss' (like 'glass' in the poem) and pluralise these. What is the difference? ('es' must be added.) Consider words ending in 'f' or 'fe' (like 'shelf', 'knife'); consonant plus 'y' (like 'sky'); 'o' (like 'potato'). Pluralise these.

Vocabulary extension
▶ Note the words 'streamlet' and 'droplet' in the texts. These are diminutives. Ask children to suggest other diminutives ending with 'let' or 'ling', or the names of the young of animals.

ANSWERS

Thinking back
1 When water in the sea is heated by the sun it turns into water vapour.
2 In the sky, water vapour turns into small droplets of water which form clouds.
3 When the clouds pass over hills or mountains they drop rain.
4 The water is carried back in streams or rivers.

Thinking about it
1 (open answer)
2 a) chills: makes cooler or colder
b) condenses: makes denser or more concentrated, turning, for example, into droplets of water (or rain).
c) commences: begins or starts
3 The name given to a small stream is streamlet.
4 a) haze b) gradually c) greets
5 A small drop of water is called a droplet.

Thinking it through
1 (open answer)
2 There is an arrow and a label telling you where to begin. There are arrows showing you the direction in which to read.
3 (open answer)
4 (open answer)
5 The purpose of the labels in the diagram is to explain each part of the process briefly and clearly and to indicate the point at which each happens in the cycle.
6 The poem is written in verse, the diagram labels are written in prose.

⇨ *Copymaster* **Flow Diagrams**
The Water Cycle is presented in the form of a flow diagram. This copymaster gives a set of instructions for children to sequence in flow diagram format.

Flow Diagrams

Name _____ *Date* _____

Here are the instructions for boiling an egg – but they are in the wrong order. Cut them out and put them in the correct order.

Write some instructions for making beans on toast. Draw some more boxes if you need to.

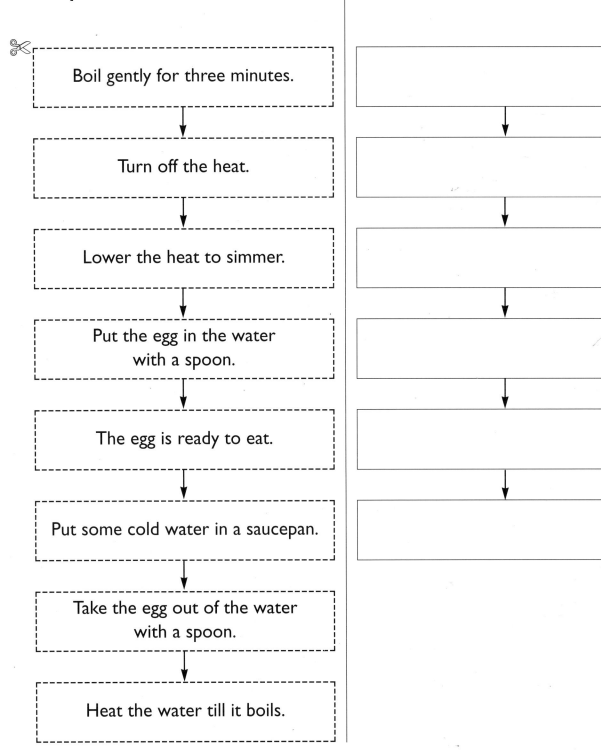

Boil gently for three minutes.

↓

Turn off the heat.

↓

Lower the heat to simmer.

↓

Put the egg in the water with a spoon.

↓

The egg is ready to eat.

↓

Put some cold water in a saucepan.

↓

Take the egg out of the water with a spoon.

↓

Heat the water till it boils.

Book 3 / Copymaster / Unit 1

Focus on Comprehension Teacher's Book 'C'   Text © Louis Fidge 1999 Illustrations © Nelson 1999   Published by Thomas Nelson and Sons Ltd

FURTHER TEACHING OPPORTUNITIES

Text level

Reading comprehension
▶ Discuss the effectiveness of the opening paragraph. Does it arouse curiosity and create a desire to read on?
▶ Ask the children how the author builds up tension as the story unfolds.
▶ Discuss how most stories have an opening, a build-up, some sort of dilemma, problem or crisis, and a resolution. How does this passage fit the pattern?
▶ Does the writer succeed in getting children to empathise with the two characters? How? Have the children ever been in any frightening situations?

Writing composition
▶ Discuss why TV writers often employ the technique of 'cliff-hangers' in serials. Encourage the children to write the next section of the story themselves.

Sentence level

Grammatical awareness
▶ Select a range of sentences from the text. Experiment by re-ordering the words to change the internal structure of the sentence, whilst trying to retain the same meaning. (A few words may be added or deleted if necessary.)

Sentence construction and punctuation
▶ Find all the verbs in the passage. What tense are they in? Discuss why. (They are all in the past tense except when Colin is thinking to himself.)

Word level

Spelling
▶ Use the text for a 'letter pattern' hunt. Select several key letter patterns for the children to focus on, such as 'oo', 'oa', 'ea', 'ow'. Ask children to search the passage and list all examples of words that include these patterns. Classify and study the sets of words.

Vocabulary extension
▶ Select words from the passage and ask children to use a thesaurus to find synonyms for them.

Ask them to explain the differences and shades of meaning between them and to compose sentences using each appropriately.

ANSWERS

Thinking back
Colin woke up and discovered Susan's bed was empty.
Susan was sleep-walking towards the quarry.
Colin ran to the edge of the cliff but could not see Susan.
Something grabbed Colin's ankle.
Colin looked down and saw a hand clutching a ledge.

Thinking about it
1 (open answer)
2 Colin couldn't understand because there was a nine foot drop from her bedroom window to the ground and the door downstairs was bolted.
3 Colin recognised Susan's pyjamas.
4 (open answer)
5 Colin could see because the moon was out.
6 Colin didn't shout to warn Susan because she was sleep-walking and it would have been dangerous to wake her.
7 (open answer)

Thinking it through
1 (open answer)
2 Colin 'ran as hard as he had ever run'. He had 'halved the lead that Susan had gained'.
3 (open answer)
4 a) silhouette: a dark shadow or outline against a lighter background
  b) quarry: a huge hole in the ground from which stones or rocks have been excavated
  c) tarn: a small mountain lake
5 (open answer)   6 (open answer)
7 Susan is literally left hanging from a cliff and the passage ends in an exciting way, leaving the story unfinished.

▷ *Copymaster* **Predictions**
Here the children are encouraged to interact with texts and to develop the ability to predict. This copymaster may be used with any reading book.

⇨ Predictions

Name _____   Date _____

1 Choose any reading book.

Title _____

Author _____

2 Look at the front cover and read the book blurb on the back cover.
Write what you think the story is going to be about.

_____

_____

3 Read the first chapter. Name the main characters.

_____

_____

Write what they are like.

_____

_____

4 Write what you think the rest of the story will be about.

_____

_____

5 Write how you think the story will end.

_____

_____

6 Read the rest of the book. Write whether your predictions were right or not.

_____

_____

7 Write what you thought of the book.

_____

_____

Book 3 / Copymaster / Unit 2

Focus on Comprehension Teacher's Book 'C'   Text © Louis Fidge 1999 Illustrations © Nelson 1999   Published by Thomas Nelson and Sons Ltd

FURTHER TEACHING OPPORTUNITIES

Text level

Reading comprehension

▶ Discuss how, at night-time, things can take on a different perspective: the sound of the wind, a creaking stair, a harmless shadow can all seem menacing and frightening. Why is this? Ask the children whether they think the things described in the poem really happened, or whether the poem is about fears at night?

▶ The poem's theme is frightening, but it also incorporates several powerful words. Ask the children to suggest what they are. How does the way the poet writes some words make them more effective?

Writing composition

▶ Do some work on metaphors. Ask children to liken the wind, or the night, to some kind of animal: for example, the wind is a wounded lion, howling in pain, lashing out at anything in its path.

Sentence level

Grammatical awareness

▶ Look at the poem critically for connectives and conjunctions, words and phrases, that sequence it and give it cohesion, such as 'one', 'that night', 'all at once'. Discuss the role they play.

Sentence construction and punctuation

▶ Punctuation marks are especially vital in poetry, providing signposts for the reader on how to tackle the text and gain meaning from it. Go through the poem again, identifying each punctuation mark and ask children to explain how it helps. (Notice particularly where some lines end with a comma and some don't, and the effect this has when reading.)

Word level

Spelling

▶ Study the poem for words containing 'o'. List these. Classify them into sets according to whether 'o' can be sounded in its own right, as in 'over', or whether it works with another letter (as a phoneme) to give it a different sound, as in 'found', 'toe', 'growled'. Discuss the number of different sound values it can have.

Vocabulary extension

▶ Select some of the verbs from the poem and ask children to supply suitable adverbs to go with them: for example, 'the wind began to moan loudly, softly, wildly, menacingly'.

ANSWERS

Thinking back

1 The woman found a <u>hairy toe</u>.
2 The wind began to <u>moan and groan</u>.
3 The woman was <u>in bed</u>.
4 The woman thought she heard <u>a voice</u>.
5 Something began to <u>creep over the floor</u>.
6 The woman could almost feel the thing <u>bending over her bed</u>.

Thinking about it

1 (open answer)   2 (open answer)
3 You can tell the woman was scared by the voice because she 'scrooched down under the covers and pulled them tight around her head'.
4 (open answer)   5 (open answer)

Thinking it through

1 (open answer)
2 (open answer) It could mean that at night-time things seem very different and it easy to imagine strange things.
3 (open answer) It is probably best spoken so that you can put expression into your voice and make it sound really scary!
4 (open answer)
5 a) (open answer)   b) (open answer)

▷ Copymaster   A Ghostly ABC

The copymaster contains an alphabetic poem on a ghostly theme. It can be used to compare with the poem in the unit, to read for enjoyment and to stimulate writing.

A Ghostly ABC

Name _____   Date _____

A for an apparition that appears without arms,

B for a black rat that blunders and alarms.

C for a cockroach that creeps into your brain,

D for Dracula drinking blood from a vein.

E for an eerie echo extended in the mind,

F for a face that floats in front and behind.

G for the ghost that glides all ghastly white,

H for the cry of HELP! in a hopeless fright.

I for the icy invisible hand of fear,

J for the jitters and the jangling chains you hear.

K for the kookaburra laughing fit to kill,

L for the lopsided leer that gives a thrill.

M for midnight when magic is abroad,

N for nightmares and the nervous tightening chord.

O for the owl, silent ghost of the dark,

P for the phantom whose footprints leave no mark.

Q for the quagmire that quivers and quakes,

R for repulsive rats and rattlesnakes.

S for the spectre that screams and sighs,

T for the tarantula that terrifies.

U for the unearthly UFO,

V for the vampires who vanish below.

W for the werewolf who wails at the moon,

X for the X-ray of a skeleton's bones.

Y for a yell and a yawning moan,

Z for a zombie from the twilight zone.

Sandy Brownjohn

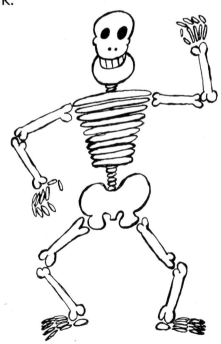

Focus on Comprehension Teacher's Book 'C'   Illustrations © Nelson 1999   Published by Thomas Nelson and Sons Ltd

FURTHER TEACHING OPPORTUNITIES

Text level

Reading comprehension
▶ Ask children how we learn what each character is like, for example by description of appearance, things they say and do. How do the children respond to each character? What are their feelings towards them? How do they think the two characters relate to each other?
▶ Discuss in what sense the story can be considered a parable or a fable.

Writing composition
▶ Ask the children to imagine the ferryman was able to telephone a friend, and to rewrite the story from his point of view, in the first person.

Sentence level

Grammatical awareness
▶ Select sentences from the passage and write them incorrectly, in non-standard English: for example, 'The old ferryman didn't never grumble.' Ask children to explain the mistakes and to rewrite the sentences in standard English.

Sentence construction and punctuation
▶ Use the text to revise the use of speech marks and the conventions associated with them, by reference to the examples in the text.

Word level

Spelling
▶ Find examples of words in the text with 'wa' or 'wo' in them, such as 'was', 'world'. Point out how the pronunciation of the 'a' and 'o' is affected. Ask children to use a dictionary to find and list other examples. Use these as a basis for spelling practice.

Vocabulary extension
▶ Find examples of compound words in the story, such as briefcase, ferryman. Provide children with the first part of some compound words and ask them to think of as many compound words as possible beginning with that word: for example, foot (ball, path, step, fall).

ANSWERS

Thinking back
1 The ferryman carried people across the River Ganges in his boat.
2 One day a well-dressed man (professor) wanted to cross the river.
3 The man carried a briefcase.
4 The man asked the ferryman if he had ever studied science.
5 The ferryman explained that he had never been to school.
6 The man told the ferryman that he was a scientist.
7 Suddenly the weather got worse (stormy).
8 The boat began to sink.

Thinking about it
1 The River Ganges is in India.
2 He was old. He ferried people across the river. He liked his job. He never grumbled. He was not wealthy or educated (he had never been to school). He could swim.
3 He liked his job because he never had to hurry and he had time to think.
4 He was well-dressed and carried a briefcase. He was a scientist. He was rather pompous. He could not swim.
5 (open answer) The ferryman knew about everyday science in the world around him, like the sun and the moon and how things worked, but he had never read any books.
6 (open answer)

Thinking it through
1 (open answer) The professor was rather narrow-minded and pompous. He had little thought for the ferryman's feelings or little understanding that knowledge does not only come from books.
2 Worthless means 'of little value'. The ferryman felt worthless because the professor made him feel as if the only sort of knowledge worth anything was that which came from books.
3 (open answer)   4 (open answer)
5 (open answer)

▶ *Copymaster* **Learning a Lesson**
This traditional story from Africa shows how we can learn from life's lessons. It is presented as a cloze procedure exercise.

⇨➔ Learning a Lesson

Name _____   *Date* _____

Think of a suitable word to fill in each gap.

Abiodun loved _____ his grandfather's
stories. 'A _____ time ago, I had a very bad
temper,' his _____ began. 'I lost a lot
_____ friends and _____ very lonely.
One day the village _____ man stopped
me. He told me he had the _____ to my
problem. He gave _____ some coloured
feathers and _____ me to go out that night
_____ place one _____ each home
in the village. He said that the next day, before
_____, I should go and collect the feathers
and take them back.'

'Did _____ do as he told you, Grandfather?' _____ asked.

'Yes I did. I placed a _____ feather outside every house. Then I went out
_____ next morning to _____ them. The problem was that _____
the night there had _____ a strong wind and they had _____ away.
I went to _____ Sepho, the wise man, and asked him to explain.'

'_____ did he say, Granfather?' Abiodum asked.

'He told me that the angry _____ I speak are like those feathers. Once
spoken they _____ be taken back. They hurt someone, and damage is
_____. It is impossible to take _____ harsh words but it is possible to
be aware of our feelings and _____ our anger.'

Abiodum smiled at his grandfather. 'Did you learn _____ lesson,
Grandfather?'

'I'm pleased to say I did, or today I would be a lonely old _____,'
he said and hugged his grandson _____.

Focus on Comprehension Teacher's Book 'C'   Text © Louis Fidge 1999 Illustrations © Nelson 1999   Published by Thomas Nelson and Sons Ltd

FURTHER TEACHING OPPORTUNITIES

Text level

Reading comprehension

▶ Find out what knowledge children have of Robin Hood, outside of the text.

▶ Ask children to create a character profile of Robin, based on information gleaned from the text (including the dialogue) or illustrations. How do Robin and Little John relate to each other? What evidence is there? How does the story portray Robin and Little John? (As good guys? As heroes? As victims?)

▶ Did children like the illustrations and 'comic book' style? How did it help understanding?

▶ Study the dialogue in the pictures. Ask children if the dialogue is designed to be humorous or serious. What words are difficult to understand? Why is this? In what sense can the story be considered a parable or a fable?

Writing composition

▶ A further 'Robin Hood' story could be written, either in continuous prose or in the same format as that in the book.

Sentence level

Grammatical awareness

▶ Ask children to write some of the dialogue from the story in the form of sentences containing direct speech. These could then be written in indirect speech, noting the changes in punctuation and words required to do so.

Sentence construction and punctuation

▶ Find examples of statements, questions, exclamations and commands in the text (in the captions or dialogue). Experiment with changing statements into questions.

Word level

Spelling

▶ Find examples of words from the text that have been suffixed in some way, for example growing, skilled, wealthy, travellers. Ask children to identify the root word in each and discuss what, if any, changes have occurred to the spelling of the root word.

Vocabulary extension

▶ Ask children to try writing some of the more archaic dialogue in modern English. Which of the words are not often used today? What do they mean?

ANSWERS

Thinking back

1 Robin Hood and his men lived in the forest.

2 Robin gave the money to the poor.

3 A tall stranger tried to cross a log bridge at the same time as Robin.

4 The giant knocked Robin into the water.

5 The tall stranger and Robin made friends.

Thinking about it

1 This means that they were fuller because they had been given a meal, but poorer because they had been robbed of their money.

2 Robin was loved by the poor because he gave them the money he had taken from the rich.

3 (open answer)

4 (open answer)

5 Robin gave three blasts on his horn to summon help.

6 The two men 'smiled with respect at each other' and were 'about to shake hands'.

Thinking it through

1 (open answer)

2 (open answer)

3 a) outlaw: someone who has broken the law

b) waylay: to lie in wait for

c) gave an inch: did not allow the other any advantage

d) stayed their hands: told his men not to grab the stranger

4 (open answer)

⇨ *Copymaster*
Robin Hood meets Little John

Children are asked to re-present the story from the unit, in the form of a playlet.

Robin Hood meets Little John

Name _____   *Date* _____

Write the story from Unit 5 as a short play. Use modern English. Include directions to the actors. Here is the start of the play. Continue on another sheet of paper if necessary.

Scene: *A broad stream in Sherwood Forest.*

Narrator: Robin is about to cross the log that spans the stream, when he sees a giant of a man about to cross from the other side, determined to go first.

Robin: *(raising his bow)* Step aside, and let me come across, or I'll shoot.

Little John: So, you would shoot a man with only a staff to defend himself, would you? That's very brave, I must say!

Robin: You stay there while I cut myself a staff – and then we'll see who's the bravest!

Narrator: Robin cuts himself a staff from a nearby tree and then returns to defend his 'log'.

_____

_____

_____

_____

_____

_____

_____

_____

Book 3 / Copymaster / Unit 5

Focus on Comprehension Teacher's Book 'C'   Text © Louis Fidge 1999   Illustrations © Nelson 1999   Published by Thomas Nelson and Sons Ltd

FURTHER TEACHING OPPORTUNITIES

Text level

Reading comprehension
- Ask children to comment on the opening sentences of the extract. Did it grab their attention and make them want to read on? Why?
- Ask children to describe their feelings about Lubber. Did they change as the story progressed? Did they see him as a victim?
- How well did the author describe the race for freedom through the Dogs' Home? Ask children to select some good descriptive words or phrases that they liked.

Writing composition
- Ask children to map out the structure of the passage, by analysing the key topic or theme in each paragraph and writing a simple sentence about it (see accompanying copymaster).

Sentence level

Grammatical awareness
- Get children to adapt the text in the book for younger readers, by reducing its length, simplifying sentences, cutting out unnecessary detail, and making the vocabulary more appropriate.

Sentence construction and punctuation
- The first sentence of the main text is interesting in that it contains verbs in the imperative present tense, a verb in the past tense and a verb in the future tense! Point out how, in the imperative 'Run for it' the pronoun 'you' is implicit. Find and read other instructional texts, such as recipes, and focus on the use of the imperative form.
- Note that some verbs require a 'helper' or auxiliary verb, as in they *will* kill. How many examples of auxiliary verbs can be found in the text?

Word level

Spelling
- Ask children to draw a chart headed one-, two- and three-syllable words. They look through the text and find a given number of examples of each. Use the words for practising syllabification, identifying syllable boundaries etc.

Vocabulary extension
- 'Run for it!' squalled Squintum (shrilly? loudly? urgently?). Discuss the use of appropriate adverbs with dialogue verbs. Provide a selection of such verbs, for example called, whispered, questioned. Ask children to suggest appropriate adverbs that could be used with each and to make up suitable sentences containing them.

ANSWERS

Thinking back
1 sleep; 2 cat; 3 follow; 4 ran; 5 excited; 6 polished; 7 rugs; 8 flap; 9 big; 10 glass

Thinking about it
1 The Dog's Home kept stray dogs for two weeks before putting them to sleep.
2 Lubber: was a big, hairy dog; was homeless; was not quick-witted; was obedient. Squintum: was the vet's Siamese cat; was quick-witted; was a fast runner; did not want Lubber killed; helped Lubber escape; knew the layout of the surgery well; used a cat flap.
3 The text says they 'stood open-mouthed'.
4 Squintum knew the Dog's Home well because he lived there.
5 (open answer)
6 They jumped back 'in startled surprise'.

Thinking it through
1 (open answer)   2 (open answer)
3 (open answer)   4 (open answer)
5 a) screamed or shouted loudly
   b) intelligent or able to respond and think quickly
   c) shattered into tiny fragments
6 (open answer)

⇨ *Copymaster*
The Bones of the Story
Children are asked to summarise the passage.

The Bones of the Story

Name _____   Date _____

Write a summary of the
passage in Unit 6. Write
one sentence in each bone.
You may use only the eight
bones to tell the story.

Lubber was about to be put to sleep by the vet.

Squintum, the vet's cat, shouted to Lubber to follow him.

Focus on Comprehension Teacher's Book 'C'   Text © Louis Fidge 1999   Illustrations © Nelson 1999   Published by Thomas Nelson and Sons Ltd

FURTHER TEACHING OPPORTUNITIES

Text level

Reading comprehension

▶ This unit contains two very different forms of text: an information text, and text containing argument and persuasive writing. After necessary explanation, ask children to find examples of the features of each type of text and discuss them. *Information texts*: written in the third person, often in fairly impersonal style; use of the present tense; lots of facts and detail; use of 'technical' terms specific to subject; use of diagrams or illustrations; clearly structured paragraphs. *Persuasive texts*: use of statistics or facts; powerful and persuasive language; the expression of personal beliefs and opinions; the use of rhetorical questions; the use of exaggeration; the use of bias.

Writing composition

▶ Discuss the importance of listening to a range of views. Ask children to write the arguments for and against wearing school uniform.

Sentence level

Grammatical awareness

▶ Use the sentences in the information text to investigate word order, by examining how far the order of the words in the sentences can be changed. Which words are essential to meaning? Which can be deleted without affecting the meaning?

Sentence construction and punctuation

▶ Commas are used in the information text for separating clauses and to separate items in a list. Find examples of both in the text. Draw attention to the use of brackets for providing additional information or explanation, and the use of a hyphen for joining together two words, especially when used as adjectives, as in white-tipped.

Word level

Spelling

▶ Select a number of tricky words from the unit. Write these on the board. Ask children to suggest ways of remembering their spellings.

Vocabulary extension

▶ Ask children to make up their own definitions for words taken from the passage and to check these against their meanings in dictionaries.

ANSWERS

Thinking back
Facts about the Red Fox
Length: 120 cm   Height: 40 cm   Weight: 10 kg
Distinctive features: dog-like appearance, pointed ears, narrow muzzle, bushy, white-tipped tail, reddish brown colour, white chest and stomach
Name of home: den
Food eaten: rodents, larger animals, fruit
Usual habitat: places where there is plenty of cover

Thinking about it
1 It appeared in a newspaper or magazine, because it appears on the 'Editor's Page'.
2 (open answer)
3 They are all about whether foxes are pests or not and whether they should be hunted.
4 (open answer)
5 The letters in favour of fox-hunting are the first and third letters.
6 Mrs Duckworth and Mr Harris are against fox-hunting.
7 (open answer)   8 (open answer)

Thinking it through
1 (open answer)
2 The letter by Mr Kirkham uses facts and figures as persuasion.
3 Views in favour of fox-hunting: foxes are a pest; they steal chickens and raid dustbins; they serve no useful purpose; there are too many foxes; hunting provides a means of sport; it is not unnecessarily cruel.
Views against fox-hunting: all life should be protected; nature has its own way of controlling population; it is cruel.

⤵ *Copymaster*   **For and Against**
This copymaster encourages children to consider the pros and cons of having a pet dog and then to state their own views in a structured manner.

⇨ For and Against

Name _____   Date _____

It is important always to consider both sides of an argument, before making up your own mind. Here are a few things people say about having a pet dog. Think of as many more things as possible to support each of the following points of view.

In favour of having a pet dog	Against having a pet dog
• Dogs can be good fun.	• They are expensive to keep.
• They provide good company.	• They are expensive to feed.
• They frighten off burglars.	• They need lots of exercise – and that takes lots of time.
_____	_____
_____	_____
_____	_____
_____	_____
_____	_____
_____	

Now you have considered both points of view,
write and say what *you* think and give *your* reasons.

Although some people say _____

I believe that _____

because _____

_____

_____

_____

_____

Focus on Comprehension Teacher's Book 'C'   Text © Louis Fidge 1999   Illustrations © Nelson 1999   Published by Thomas Nelson and Sons Ltd

FURTHER TEACHING OPPORTUNITIES

Text level

Reading comprehension

- What do the children think was the purpose of the interview? Why do famous people agree to be interviewed like this?
- What was the most interesting thing Gary said?
- What other questions could have been asked?
- Ask children to collect and read a wide range of magazine and newspaper interviews and identify common features.

Writing composition

- Ask children to imagine they were invited to the interview and ask them to write a report of it to a good friend, explaining what they saw and did, and what they enjoyed and felt.

Sentence level

Grammatical awareness

- The interview could be used to practise recording direct speech, reinforcing the appropriate conventions of punctuation. Sentences could then be translated in to indirect speech and differences discussed.

Sentence construction and punctuation

- Use the text as an opportunity to discuss the differences between written language and the spoken word, including conventions used to guide the reader, the need for writing to make sense away from the immediate context, and the use of punctuation to replace intonation, pauses and gestures.

Word level

Spelling

- Gary is a musician. Think of other words using the same suffix 'ian'. Find words in the text with the following suffixes: 'al', 'ness', 'ous', 'tion', 'ment'. Ask children to think of other words with the same suffixes.
- Ask children to brainstorm and list words to do with people with the suffixes 'er', (singer), 'or' (actor), 'ar' (vicar).

Vocabulary extension

- Gary mentions quite a few 'technical' words related to the music business. Find these in the text and ask children to define them. Encourage children to collect other words related to the same theme.

ANSWERS

Thinking back

1 Gary Goldwater.
2 Gary is a pop star.
3 He formed his first band at college.
4 His first show was difficult.
5 His most exciting memory is flying across the Atlantic in Concorde.
6 He says you need determination to succeed.

Thinking about it

1 Their van broke down and they arrived very late. One of the microphones packed up. The drummer lost one of his drumsticks. Gary knocked an amplifier over. During their act the electricity went out.
2 They flew across the Atlantic in Concorde. They met some famous film stars in Hollywood.
3 (open answer) 4 (open answer)
5 a) mime: act or mimic without words
b) turning professional: making a living as a pop group
c) amplify: to make louder
d) unscrupulous: dishonest.

Thinking it through

1 (open answer) 2 (open answer)
3 (open answer) 4 (open answer)

Copymaster **Facts and Opinions**

The skill of differentiating fact from opinion is focused on in this copymaster.

Facts and Opinions

Name _____   Date _____

1 Write whether you think each of these statements is a fact or an opinion.

Manchester United is wonderful.

Edinburgh is a city in Scotland.

July comes after June.

_____   _____   _____

Mount Everest is a high mountain.

Yellow is the best colour.

I think tennis is great!

_____   _____   _____

2 Write your opinions. Afterwards compare your answers with a friend's. Explain and justify your opinions.

Which is the most enjoyable sport?   Which is the fiercest animal?

_____   _____

Which crisps are nicest?   Which subject at school is best?

_____   _____

Which is the funniest TV programme?   What is the tastiest fruit?

_____   _____

3 Which is your favourite band? How would you persuade someone the are best? Make a list of some points you would make. Say after each, whether it is a fact or opinion.

_____

_____

_____

Focus on Comprehension Teacher's Book 'C'   Text © Louis Fidge 1999 Illustrations © Nelson 1999   Published by Thomas Nelson and Sons Ltd

FURTHER TEACHING OPPORTUNITIES

Text level

Reading comprehension
▶ Discuss memories and why some stay vivid in our minds, whilst others just disappear. Talk about how early memories are often fragmented and partial. Relate this to the poem. How do we know this was the case with the girl? Why does she keep repeating 'so long ago'?
▶ Discuss in what way this is a very 'personal' poem, rooted in the child's experiences. How is it also very much to do with the child's sensory perception?
▶ Ask children to express their opinions of the content and style of the poem.
▶ Note the way the poem is structured (in verses, three lines per verse, rhyming).

Writing composition
▶ Ask children to recall vivid memories from when they were young and to record them, modelled on the form of the poem.

Sentence level

Grammatical awareness
▶ Use the text to revise work on nouns. Ask children to find examples of nouns in the text. Try reading sentences from the passage again and leaving the nouns out to focus on their function.

Sentence construction and punctuation
▶ Translate the poem into prose, breaking up the long sentences into short ones, yet retaining the essence of the meaning: for example, I dragged on the dusty road. I remember seeing an old woman. She was looking over the fence at me...'

Word level

Spelling
▶ Focus on the word 'hummed' from the poem. The root word is 'hum' When suffixed what happens? Ask children to think of other verbs ending with a consonant, preceded by a short vowel, for example sit, beg, tap, shop. Which words can take 'ing'? 'ed'? Which can be made into nouns with 'er'?
▶ Do the same with adjectives, such as hot, wet, red. Compare them in, for example, hot, hotter, hottest.

Vocabulary extension
▶ Which of the words in the poem have antonyms (opposites)? Point out examples, such as remember – forget, over – under. Write them, with their antonyms. What part of speech (say, noun or verb) is each word?

ANSWERS

Thinking back
1 The road was long and dusty.
2 The poet was three years old.
3 The old woman asked if the child liked bilberries and cream for tea.
4 The cat purred.
5 She was wearing a red shawl.

Thinking about it
1 'Long ago' means many years in the past, when the poet was a child of three.
2 a) The poet remembers the sounds of the old lady calling out, the old woman humming, the cat purring.
b) The poet remembers the taste of bilberries and cream.
c) The poet remembers the smell of everything that used to be.
3 The poet talks about 'the feel of the sun' and the 'heat on the road'.
4 (open answer)   5 (open answer)

Thinking it through
1 (open answer)
2 (open answer)
3 (open answer)
4 (open answer)

▷ *Copymaster*   **What's in a Memory?**
Two different poems on the theme of memories are provided to read and discuss, and to compare and contrast with the poem in the unit.

What's in a Memory?

Name _____   *Date* _____

Memories

Memories – lying in the murky
            recesses of my mind.
Memories – silently sleeping,
            slumbering uneasily.
Memories – snapshots of the past,
            some blurred – some razor sharp.
Memories – cameos of my personal history,
            crucially moulding who I am.
Memories – they're all there – just there
            waiting patiently – waiting,
            just waiting to be woken.

Anon.

Grandma

'I remember
when I could sunfill my face
with fields of cowslips.'

Her eyes glazed
As she reflected her girlhood.
And I longed to butter my chin
With the wild flowers of her youth.

Later that year
We took her to hidden
Country depths
And by the roadside,
Fullcreamed and flourishing,
The cowslips bunched
On untouched banks.

'See, see,' she cried,
'That's *just* how it used to be!'

Anita Marie Sackett

Focus on Comprehension Teacher's Book 'C'   Illustrations © Nelson 1999   Published by Thomas Nelson and Sons Ltd

FURTHER TEACHING OPPORTUNITIES

Text level

Reading comprehension

▶ Before reading the story in the unit ask children to recall the traditional version of the story. After reading the story identify similarities and differences with the original. Consider how the story has changed over time and identify the distinctive cultural influences on the modern version.

▶ Discuss the fact that many old stories were passed on orally before the advent of books. What are the advantages and disadvantages of this? Ask children to re-tell the story in the unit from memory. How true to the text in the passage was it? Explore the similarities and differences between oral and written story telling.

Writing composition

▶ Ask children to make the story into a play script.

Sentence level

Grammatical awareness

▶ Identify all the pronouns in the story. Ask children which nouns they stand for. Try reading the text, substituting the relevant noun instead of the pronoun to show how pronouns help avoid much repetition.

Sentence construction and punctuation

▶ Provide children with some 'telegraphic' sentences based on the text: for example, New York – beautiful girl – Snow White. Ask children to flesh these out into proper sentences.

Word level

Spelling

▶ Use the word 'beautiful' to show that the suffix 'ful' drops one 'l' when added to a word. Ask children to suggest a number of adjectives ending in 'ful' and write them both ways: for example beautiful = full of beauty. Which of the root words change their spelling when 'ful' is added (for example, mercy = merciful)?

Vocabulary extension

▶ Investigate antonyms. Why do some words (such as 'down') have only one opposite while others (such as 'little') have more than one, and others (such as 'music') have none? Study some of the words in the text to see which class they fall in.

ANSWERS

Thinking back

1 lived; 2 married; 3 jealous; 4 bodyguards; 5 shoot; 6 left; 7 jazz-men; 8 sang; 9 reporter; 10 picture; 11 Mirror; 12 held; 13 honour; 14 kill; 15 poisoned

Thinking about it

1 Being both poor and rich could mean that she was rich in terms of money, but poor in the sense that she was to be pitied because of what happened to her.
2 (open answer)
3 The New York Mirror was really a newspaper. The story talks of a reporter from the paper and Snow White's picture appearing on its front page.
4 The step-mother was jealous of Snow White because she was more beautiful than she was.
5 The seven jazz-men worked in a club.
6 When she sang at the club a newspaper reporter took a picture of her, for his newspaper.
7 (open answer)
8 When the jazz-men stumbled whilst carrying Snow White's coffin, it dislodged the poisoned cherry from her throat.

Thinking it through

1 (open answer)   2 (open answer)
3 (open answer)   4 (open answer)
5 (open answer)

⇨ *Copymaster*
   The Hare and the Tortoise
Part of the traditional story is re-told in a modern version here. Children are asked to finish the story in their own words.

30

The Hare and the Tortoise

Name _____   Date _____

The crowds buzzed with excitement as they gathered at the starting point. Vendors were there selling soft drinks and fast food. Promoters were there giving away free samples of their products. News reporters and technicians were there to capture every moment of the event for the viewers.

The hare stepped forward and took off his pink warm-up suit with a flourish. He waved to his fans and flashed a sparkling smile to the cameras. He snarled at the tortoise out of the side of his mouth, 'I'm going to show you up so much, you'll wish you had never been born!'

The starter held up his arm for the start of the race. (He was not allowed to use a pistol because firearms were banned.) On the signal to go, the hare was off in a lightning blaze of speed. The tortoise ambled off slowly. He knew that most sports injuries are caused by abrupt starts and lack of preparation.

The crowds cheered as the hare rushed on. He had soon left the tortoise far behind. So confident was he of winning that he agreed to stop and give the television reporters an interview about his mid-race thoughts, his childhood memories and his hopes for the future.

Meanwhile the tortoise ambled on, taking frequent drinks to prevent him from becoming dehydrated …

1   List the clues that tell you this is a modern version of the traditional story.

    _____

    _____

    _____

2   What can you learn about the characters of the hare and tortoise?

    _____

    _____

    _____

3   Are their characters any different from those in the traditional version
    of the story? _____

4   On another sheet of paper (or the other side of this sheet), finish the story
    in the same style as above.

Book 3 / Copymaster / Unit 10

Focus on Comprehension Teacher's Book 'C'   Text © Louis Fidge 1999   Illustrations © Nelson 1999   Published by Thomas Nelson and Sons Ltd

FURTHER TEACHING OPPORTUNITIES

Text level

Reading comprehension

▶ One of the features of explanatory texts is the use of words and phrases (such as 'while', 'during', 'after') to make causal, logical connections. Find examples of such language in the text.

Writing composition

▶ With the class, use the text as a means for showing children how to use simple abbreviations when making notes, and in deciding which are the key points to note.

Sentence level

Grammatical awareness

▶ Ask children to find examples of different types of nouns in the text: for example, common nouns like 'world', 'mouth'; proper nouns like 'Europe', 'Hansel' and 'Gretel'; abstract nouns like 'good' and 'evil'; collective nouns like 'collections of stories'. Think of other examples of each. Discuss the differences between the types of nouns. Discuss the functions of nouns. Which of the nouns are singular? plural? What gender are the nouns?

Sentence construction and punctuation

▶ Discuss how well the headings summarise the key theme of each section.

▶ Look in newspapers and magazines at the headlines. These are often sentence contractions. Is the meaning clear? Do they use plays on words? Do they contain ambiguities, as in 'Police shot man with knife'?

Word level

Spelling

▶ Discuss the word 'once' from the text. Draw attention to the soft sound of the 'c'. This usually occurs when the 'c' is followed by 'e', 'i' or 'y'. Brainstorm words containing soft 'c'.

▶ Extend this to a consideration of the soft 'g' which is affected in much the same way (as in the word 'generation').

Vocabulary extension

▶ Just as stories travel by word of mouth, so do individual words. Our language is full of words we have 'borrowed' from other languages. Ask the children to check the etymology of these words in an etymological dictionary if possible: (from Italy) 'pizza', balcony', 'opera', piano'; (from France) 'banquet', 'biscuit'; (from India) 'bungalow', verandah', 'jungle'; (from the Middle East) 'bazaar', caravan', 'turban'.

ANSWERS

Thinking back

1 Some common themes in traditional stories are: the struggle between good and evil, rich and poor, young and old, beautiful and ugly, male and female.
2 Some common ingredients in traditional stories are: magic and supernatural, heroes and villains, animals behaving like humans, epic journeys.
3 Stories were passed on by word of mouth.
4 The first collection of stories was made by Somadeva, an Indian wise man.
5 The first Italian collector of traditional stories was Charles Perrault and the first German collectors were Jacob and Wilhelm Grimm.

Thinking about it

1 Stories were carried by travellers and were re-told in the different countries they visited.
2 (open answer)   3 (open answer)
4 (open answer)

Thinking it through

1 (open answer)   2 (open answer)
3 (open answer)
4 a) (open answer)   b) (open answer)
  c) (open answer)   d) (open answer)

⇨ *Copymaster*
The Story of Sit and Lakhan

An abbreviated form of the traditional Indian story is given. Children are asked to suggest similarities and differences between this and the story of Snow White (demonstrating how stories travel and may appear in different places in different guises).

The Story of Sit and Lakhan

Name _____   Date _____

This is a version of an old Indian story.

> Once upon a time a king had two sons called Sit and Lakhan. One sad day the king's wife died. After a while the king remarried. His second wife could not have children. She hated Sit and Lakhan and plotted to get rid of them.
>
> One day she pretended to fall desperately ill. The wicked woman told the king that she would only recover if she ates the livers of the two boys. The king was in a terrible state and did not know what to do. Eventually he agreed to their murder.
>
> Three guards were ordered to take the boys into a forest to kill them. When they got there, the guards could not bring themselves to harm the innocent children. Instead of killing them they released them and told them to run. The guards killed two dogs and returned to the palace with their livers instead.
>
> Sit and Lakhan were left to wander through the forest. At dusk they rescued two small birds from a snake. The grateful parents of the birds threw down pieces of magical food to the boys. Whoever ate the first piece would marry the daughter of a rich raja (like a king), and whoever ate the second piece would spit gold …

The story continues and eventually ends with happiness for both the boys. Their father and step-mother get their just punishment.

List all the similarities and differences to the traditional story of Snow White.

Similarities	Differences

Focus on Comprehension Teacher's Book 'C'   Text © Louis Fidge 1999 Illustrations © Nelson 1999   Published by Thomas Nelson and Sons Ltd

FURTHER TEACHING OPPORTUNITIES

Text level

Reading comprehension

▶ Ask children to suggest the main theme of the poem: for example, a discussion of what God is like. Ask children to suggest why people have such different views of God.

▶ Ask children what sort of things they argue over. Get them to suggest different ways of resolving arguments. In the poem, how did the seventh voice defuse the tension?

Writing composition

▶ The poem uses figurative language and metaphors, such as 'God is laughter.' Ask children to suggest natural things (such as fog) and describe them, using similes or metaphors: for example, 'Fog is like an old man with a long, wispy white beard' or 'Fog is a robber, sneaking quietly around at night while everyone is asleep.'

Sentence level

Grammatical awareness

▶ The poem is written in West Indian patois, in which there is not always agreement between subject and verb, or consistency of verb tenses. Ask children to find examples of this and to suggest how it might be written in standard English.

Sentence construction and punctuation

▶ Poets often deliberately use licence with punctuation for effect. Does this matter? Read the poem again, and ask the children to suggest where punctuation has been omitted.

Word level

Spelling

▶ Write the words 'snow and mother' from the text on the board. Then write 'now and moth' next to them. Discuss how words may contain the same letter patterns but be pronounced differently. Ask children to think of other examples: (rough/cough; spook/cook; headache/moustache).

Vocabulary extension

▶ The poem is set by the sea. Use this to explore relevant onomatopoeic words (whose meanings are represented in their sounds) like 'splash, plop, whoosh'. Ask children to suggest others. Invent words if necessary. Extend this to words related to sounds in general: for example, traffic words, engine noises.

ANSWERS

Thinking back

1 the clouds are so fluffy and sheepy.
2 the rain falls in strands.
3 the night is dark.
4 of the colour of snow.

Thinking about it

1 The second and the sixth voice thought God was a man.
2 The third and fifth voice thought God was a woman.
3 (open answer)
4 The seventh person thinks God might be like a story with no beginning or end, or like laughter.
5 (open answer)

Thinking it through

1 It rhymes in many places so it is more like a poem than a play.
2 (open answer)   3 (open answer)
4 (open answer)
5 a) The words that are spoken are written in italics.
   b) Words that a narrator might say (that tell the story) are in capitals. Some words are also put in capitals to emphasise them.
6 (open answer)

▷▶ *Copymaster* **Pollution**
This poem is in the form of a conversation (like that in the unit) between a mother and child. It should be read and discussed and compared with the poem in the unit.

Pollution

Name _____   Date _____

'Mummy, Oh Mummy, what's this pollution
That everyone's talking about?'
'Pollution's the mess that the country is in,
That we'd all be far better off without.
It's factories belching their fumes in the air,
And the beaches all covered with tar,
Now throw all those sweet papers into the bushes
Before we get back into the car.'

'Mummy, Oh Mummy, who makes pollution,
And why don't they stop if it's bad?'
'Cos people like that just don't think about others,
They don't think at all, I might add.
They spray all the crops and poison the flowers,
And wipe out the birds and the bees,
Now there's a good place we could dump that old mattress
Right out of sight in the trees.'

'Mummy, Oh Mummy, what's going to happen
If all the pollution goes on?'
Well the world will end up like a second-hand junk yard,
With all its treasures quite gone.
The fields will be littered with plastics and tins,
The streams will be covered with foam,
Now throw those two bottles over the hedge,
Save us from carting them home.'

'But Mummy, Oh Mummy, if I throw the bottles,
Won't that be polluting the wood?'
'Nonsense! that isn't the same thing at all,
You just shut up and be good.
If you're going to start getting silly ideas
I'm taking you home right away,
'Cos pollution is something that other folks do,
We're just enjoying our day.'

Anon.

Book 3 / Copymaster / Unit 12

Focus on Comprehension Teacher's Book 'C'   Text © Louis Fidge 1999   Illustrations © Nelson 1999   Published by Thomas Nelson and Sons Ltd

FURTHER TEACHING OPPORTUNITIES

Text level

Reading comprehension

▶ Draw attention to the fact that this text is clearly divided into three main elements: the 'you will need' section, the diagrams and the written instructions (what you do).

▶ Discuss how the diagrams help the reader. What function do they serve?

▶ Ask children why the instructions are sequenced in steps and written separately.

▶ Ask children to suggest any ways in which the instructions could have been improved.

Writing composition

▶ Pick a fairly simple game, such as noughts and crosses, and ask children to write instructions for playing the game. Ask them to test the instructions by following them exactly to see if they are easy to understand, and if anything has been missed. Evaluate their writing in terms of its a) purpose b) organisation and layout c) clarity.

Sentence level

Grammatical awareness

▶ Ask children to rewrite a section of the text, but delete every, say, seventh or tenth word, writing it as a cloze passage. How difficult is it to read? How easy is it for someone else to guess the missing words? Analyse what function each deleted word plays: is it a noun, a verb?

Sentence construction and punctuation

▶ Discuss the fact that instructions are usually written like commands or orders, (in the imperative) telling you what to do, but that the pronoun 'you' is not used (it is implicit). Note, too, that the instructions are all written in the present tense (telling you what to do).

Word level

Spelling

▶ Use the text to study words ending in vowels. Find all the words in this category. Which vowel is most commonly used? By brainstorming and looking in books, come up with lists of words ending in vowels other than 'e'. Invent new words ending in vowels other than 'e'.

Vocabulary extension

▶ Look at the word 'scissors'. Is it singular or plural? Ask the children to think of other words like this. (Note that they can often be preceded by 'a pair of ...', as in trousers, glasses.)

ANSWERS

Thinking back

1 The instructions tell you how to make an identi-flick book.
2 Eight sheets of A4 paper, stapler, ruler, pair of scissors, pens and pencils for drawing/colouring.
3 There are eight steps in the process.
4 DON'T CUT THE FRONT OR BACK COVERS!
5 There are five points listed.

Thinking about it

1 Step 1   2 Step 3   3 Step 4
4 Steps 2, 6 and 7
5 You have to draw a different face on every page so that when you flick through the book you can make lots of different combinations of faces.
6 You make different identi-kit faces with your book by turning back different strips from different faces.

Thinking it through

1 a) It is easier to make the book if you have got together all the things you need first.
   b) This helps to separate the items and makes it clear how many items are needed.
2 a) (open answer)   b) (open answer)
   c) (open answer)
3 Capital letters emphasise the words.

⇨ Copymaster
Following Instructions

A selection of items from a mail order catalogue, along with their descriptions, is given. Children are asked to choose four items, and, using the information provided, fill in an order form.

Following Instructions

Name _____   *Date* _____

**Choose four items from this page from a mail order catalogue.
Fill in the order form as if you were ordering them.**

DEAR DIARY
- Compact
- 18 functions
- Stores names, addresses and birthdays
- Scheduler/memo facility
- Likes/dislikes and secrets/wishes
- Secret password function

Cat. No. 360/4630
£19.75

YOUNG SCIENTIST BINOCULARS
Smooth focusing
7 x 25 mm magnification.
Robust.
Cat. No. 350/5643
£7.99

'SMART START' PREMIER PLUS
22 built-in activities. Teaches letters, spelling, numbers, maths, logic and memory games. 3 skill levels. Suitable for 2 players. Requires 4 x AA batteries.
Cat No. 360/5811
£33.50

EASY IN-LINE SKATES
Designed to make in-line skating easy. Advanced skaters can remove lock for free-wheeling fun.
Cat. No. 366/1518
£17.75

WALKIE TALKIE PHONES
2 portable phone style walkie talkies with folding mouthpiece. 100 m range in free field and morse code facility.
Cat. No. 354/9025
£14.99

MAIL ORDER COMPANY

Please send me:

Cat. No.	Goods	Quantity	Size	Price	Total

I enclose a cheque, money order, or cash. (Delete as necessary.)
If I am not satisified with my goods, I may return them within 30 days for a refund.

Print your full name and address:
Mr/Mrs/Miss/Ms _____
Address _____
_____ Postcode_____

Focus on Comprehension Teacher's Book 'C'   Text © Louis Fidge 1999 Illustrations © Nelson 1999   Published by Thomas Nelson and Sons Ltd

FURTHER TEACHING OPPORTUNITIES

Text level

Reading comprehension

▶ Ask children to try to explain what a myth is. (A myth is an ancient traditional story of gods or heroes which addresses a problem or concern of human experience.) Ask children to suggest where this myth is from and to give their reasons.

▶ Ask children for their response to the myth as a whole. Did they like it?

▶ Summarise some of the characteristics of myths and look for evidence of each in the story: they involve gods and goddesses; they have events with supernatural happenings; they involve evil doings; they take place in a different culture, long ago.

Writing composition

▶ Ask children to make up their own myth, explaining how the evils of the world came into being. Remind them of the features of myths.

Sentence level

Grammatical awareness

▶ Use the passage as an opportunity to revise work on different classes of words (parts of speech). Select one (say, prepositions) and ask children to identify all examples they can find in the text, and to explain the function they serve.

Sentence construction and punctuation

▶ The passage has several simple, short sentences. Ask children to extend each, by adding other clauses or phrases, and making them into longer, complex sentences by using connectives and conjunctions. Reinforce the use of commas in punctuating these sentences.

Word level

Spelling

▶ Look for words in the passage that could be written other ways and yet still retain the same pronunciation (homophones): for example, there, their, they're. Ask children to list these. Have a competition to see who can come up with the most.

Vocabulary extension

▶ Ask children to find and list all the adjectives in the text. Get them to think of at least one antonym (opposite) for each, and more if possible. Were there any for which this was not possible? Why?

ANSWERS

Thinking back

1 Prometheus trapped nasty things in a box.
2 Prometheus gave the box to Epimetheus.
3 Jupiter sent Pandora to Epimetheus as a gift.
4 Pandora promised not to open the box.
5 Pandora broke her promise.
6 Pandora allowed the nasty things to escape.
7 The only thing left in the box was Hope.

Thinking about it

1 a) (open answer)   b) (open answer)
  c) (open answer)
2 Prometheus stole some fire from heaven because they had none on Earth.
3 It made Jupiter angry.
4 (open answer)
5 (open answer)

Thinking it through

1 (open answer)
2 a) She opened the box and let out all the evil things.
  b) He married Pandora and was unable to prevent her from opening the box.
  c) He stole fire from heaven and made Jupiter so angry that he decided to send Pandora into the world to set the nasty things free.
  d) He sent Pandora into the world.
3 (open answer)   4 (open answer)

▶ *Copymaster*
Why Do Dogs Chase Cars?
A modern story from Ghana is provided to compare with the older story in the unit. Both set out to offer an explanation as to why things are as they are.

Why Do Dogs Chase Cars?

Name _____ Date _____

This is a modern folk story from Northern Ghana in Africa. It offers an explanation for a common everyday event in that part of the world.

Some time ago, when cars first came to the roads, a donkey, a goat and a dog took a ride in a taxi to the villages where they lived.

When they reached the first village, the donkey tapped the driver on the shoulder. 'This is where I'm getting out, driver,' he said. 'How much?'

'Three thousand francs,' said the driver.

The donkey paid up and on went the goat and dog in the taxi. Soon the goat asked to be dropped off.

'How much?' he asked.

'Three thousand francs,' said the driver.

The goat jumped from the taxi and scampered off into the bush.

At long last the dog got to where he wanted to go.

'How much?' said the dog.

'Three thousand francs,' said the driver.

The dog held up a five thousand franc note. The driver grabbed the note, and drove off down the road, roaring with laughter.

So now you know why animals all do different things when a car comes down the road.

Donkeys stay right where they are. They let the driver go round them. They know they paid up. They've done nothing wrong so they've got nothing to be ashamed of.

The moment a car comes down the road and there's a goat around, it'll scamper off as fast as it can because it knows that it didn't pay the fare and the driver is looking for his money.

But dogs spend their whole time chasing cars, looking for the driver who once cheated them.

From South and North and East and West edited by Michael Rosen

FURTHER TEACHING OPPORTUNITIES

Text level

Reading comprehension

▶ Invite children to respond to the poem. Do they like the idea of 'special things'? Did they like the poet's choice of things?

▶ Look at how the poem is structured. Does it rhyme? Does it matter?

▶ Discuss with the children in what sense the poet could be said to be 'painting pictures with words'.

▶ Invite children to collect and compile an anthology of favourite poems, with personal commentaries on each, illuminating their choices.

Writing composition

▶ Ask children to make up their own verses, using the poem as a model. After writing their first drafts, encourage them to share their ideas with others, and then refine their poems in the light of these comments.

Sentence level

Grammatical awareness

▶ The poem contains some fairly sophisticated ideas and words and is written in appropriate language, and at an appropriate readability level for Year 5 children. Ask the children to rewrite it in a simpler form, suitable for reading to Key Stage 1 children, by changing sentences structures and vocabulary.

▶ Discuss which of the verses are written in the future tense and which in the present tense. How can this be seen? What is the reason?

Sentence construction and punctuation

▶ Re-read the poem and draw attention to the use of commas separating items in a list (as in the first four verses), and to mark grammatical boundaries (as in the last two verses); and the use of the hyphen (for joining two words together when used as adjectives).

Word level

Spelling

▶ Point out the use of the silent 'u' in 'tongue'. Ask children to look up words beginning with 'gu' in a dictionary. In which words is the 'u' silent? Ask them to try to make up a rule for this.

Vocabulary extension

▶ In the 'Thinking back' section, initials were used to represent words. Ask children to suggest examples of acronyms and other abbreviations like TV which stand for longer words.

ANSWERS

Thinking back

1 a) FNCD = fire from the nostrils of a Chinese dragon
   b) SRB = a snowman with a rumbling belly
   c) LSEF = a leaping spark from an electric fish
   d) LJAU = the last joke of an ancient uncle
   e) FSB = the first smile of a baby
   f) WWH = a witch on a white horse
2 Three violet wishes will be spoken in Gujarati.
3 The box is made from ice and gold and steel, with stars on the lid and secrets in the corner. Its hinges are the toe joints of dinosaurs.
4 He will land on a yellow beach the colour of the sun.

Thinking about it

1 Gujarati is a language spoken in India.
2 (open answer)
3 a) (open answer)   b) (open answer)
4 (open answer)

Thinking it through

1 (open answer)   2 (open answer)
3 (open answer)   4 (open answer)
5 (open answer)

⇨ *Copymaster* Riddles

There is an air of magic and mystery about the poem in the unit. The traditional riddles given on this copymaster have a mystery element about them and have given countless children fun for many years. Answers: **1** a river; **2** a clock; **3** a mirror; **4** the yolk of an egg

Riddles

Name _____ Date _____

Write an answer to each riddle. Explain your reasons.

I

| Both day and night I stay in bed,
Yet never sleep or rest my head;
I have no feet to skip or hop,
And yet I run and never stop. |

Answer: _____

Reasons: _____

_____

_____

_____

2

| Some thing I tell,
With never a word;
I keep it well,
Though it flies like a bird. |

Answer: _____

Reasons: _____

_____

_____

_____

_____

3

| Hold it steady in your hand,
Then you will see another land,
Where right is left, and left is right,
And no sound stirs by day or night;
When you look in, yourself you see,
Yet in that place you cannot be. |

Answer: _____

Reasons: _____

_____

_____

_____

_____

4

| In marble halls as white as milk,
Lined with a skin as soft as silk,
Within a fountain crystal-clear,
A golden apple doth appear,
No doors there are in this
  stronghold,
Yet thieves break in and steal
  the gold. |

Answer: _____

Reasons: _____

_____

_____

_____

_____

Focus on Comprehension Teacher's Book 'C'   Text © Louis Fidge 1999 Illustrations © Nelson 1999   Published by Thomas Nelson and Sons Ltd

FURTHER TEACHING OPPORTUNITIES

Text level

Reading comprehension

▶ Have a class discussion, asking children to suggest advantages and disadvantages of school. Read the article on page 40 and then ask children what surprised them about it.

▶ After reading the letter on pupils' book page 41 ask children what sort of letter it was. How did they feel after reading it?

▶ Ask children to comment on how persuasive the advertisements are and why.

Writing composition

▶ Ask children to produce an advert for their house, using those in the newspaper as models.

Sentence level

Grammatical awareness

▶ Use the text to revise work on pronouns. Ask children to identify the pronouns, both personal and possessive, and to say who or what each pronoun stands for. Which are singular and which plural?

Sentence construction and punctuation

▶ The text on page 40 is liberally sprinkled with apostrophes, used in contractions. Ask children to find these and write each in its fuller form.

▶ The advertisements on page 41 contain possessive apostrophes. Find and discuss these.

Word level

Spelling

▶ Find examples of words from the text that have been suffixed or prefixed in some way. Ask children to identify the root word in each and discuss what, if any, changes have occurred to the spelling of the root word.

Vocabulary extension

▶ Our language has many Greek influences. Ask children to use a dictionary to find words beginning with the following Greek prefixes: 'arch', 'anti', 'auto', 'dia', 'mono', 'para', 'syl', 'tele'.

ANSWERS

Thinking back

1 Most people thought it was a bad idea.
2 It is a waste of time and money. School is no use in later life. It does not teach skills for living.
3 It sets the boys apart from the common people.
4 reading, writing, sums, music, athletics.
5 People thought girls needed to learn to spin, weave and cook in order to run a household.
6 rubbish in the streets, overcrowding, poor buildings and safety in the city.
7 A delightful country house. Spacious rooms surround a large courtyard with altar to household gods. Accommodation: luxurious men's dining room, quiet and private women's rooms, slaves' quarters. Farmland with three wells, olive groves, vineyards, grazing suitable for goats and pigs. 2 kilometres west of Delphi.

Thinking about it

1 Only sons of wealthy parents attended school.
2 They learnt their fathers' trades.
3 Some wealthy families sent their sons to school.
4 Speaking cleverly in public helped them gain more power in the Assembly.
5 Yes, because when girls grew up they should be able to run a household smoothly.
6 People thought girls needed to learn skills like spinning, weaving and cooking.
7 Because he had lived in Athens for 30 years and things had got steadily worse over that period.
8 He requested a proper collection system for litter, better building regulations, some form of policing the streets to reduce crime.
9 (open answer)

Thinking it through

1 (open answer)   2 (open answer)
3 (open answer)
4 The streets are littered with rubbish. The city is overcrowded. Some buildings are in a bad condition. Streets are narrow and twisty. Thieves and crooks hang around in them.
5 (open answer)

▣▶ *Copymaster* **Persuading People**
Children are asked to think through their views on pocket money.

⇨ **Persuading People**

Name _____   *Date* _____

Decide which of these statements you agree with.

> We have a right to pocket money. We should not have to do anything for it.

> We should do jobs to earn our pocket money.

> We should be given a set amount of pocket money. We should get more for the jobs we do.

Write your view about pocket money. _____

_____

Write several reasons why you think this. _____

_____

_____

_____

Now write some sentences persuading others why they should agree with you.

Use only the space below.

FURTHER TEACHING OPPORTUNITIES

Text level

▶ Ask children why they think the flow diagram approach was used to explain how news is collected, rather than the more conventional continuous text divided into paragraphs. How helpful is it? Why are the steps numbered?

▶ Draw attention to the features of the style and ask children to find examples of each: impersonal style; use of the passive voice; presented in the third person; use of present tense; use of 'technical' vocabulary; use of words/phrases (such as 'as soon as') to make sequential, causal links.

▶ Ask children what they notice about the sentences in the timetable on pupils' page 46. (They are in telegraphic note form.)

▶ Consider the style of the agenda (written in the form of instructions, the verbs in the imperative).

Writing composition

▶ Ask children to imagine they are the reporters at the scene of the accident. They could either write a report for their television company; write notes about what they see; or write an article for the local newspaper, with description, factual information and interviews of eye witnesses.

Sentence level

Grammatical awareness

▶ Make up some statements from 'eye witnesses' as if spoken in non-standard English: for example, 'We was just overtaking this lorry when up comes some geezer on the wrong side of the road …'. Ask children to translate the dialogue into standard English and comment on the differences.

Sentence construction and punctuation

▶ Link this with the preceding suggestion, and use it as an opportunity to discuss the differences between written language and the spoken word, including conventions used to guide the reader, the need for writing to make sense away from the immediate context, and the use of punctuation to replace intonation, pauses and gestures.

Word level

Spelling

▶ Use the verb 'arrive' from the text to study what happens to the 'e' when 'ing' or 'ed' is added. Brainstorm other verbs to which this happens. Ask children to make up a rule to cover it.

▶ Think of words with a silent 'e' which retain it when adding a suffix beginning with a consonant (for example, lively, careful).

Vocabulary extension

▶ Ask children to find a number of words from the text beginning with a particular letter, say 'c'. Ask them to list these in alphabetical order.

ANSWERS

Thinking back

1 The first people to arrive at the scene were the local police and fire brigade.
2 The local reporter informed the national TV companies.
3 The editor reads the report to decide whether to show it on the evening news or not.
4 At the 2 o'clock meeting they decide what will go into the news programme.
5 The news programme is planned at 5.30 pm.
6 The evening news is broadcast at 6 pm.

Thinking about it

1 (open answer)   2 (open answer)
3 (open answer)   4 (open answer)
5 (open answser)

Thinking it through

1 (open answer)   2 (open answer)
3 (open answer)   4 (open answer)
5 (open answer) An agenda is a list of points or issues that are to be discussed or covered in a meeting. A timetable is the order in which things are to be done and the time at which they are expected to be done.

⇨ Copymaster   Going Bananas!

A gorilla has escaped from a nearby Safari Park! Children are given the notes made by a local reporter and asked to convert them into a newspaper article.

Going Bananas!

Name _____ Date _____

A gorilla named Guy escaped from a nearby safari park
and caused chaos in the High Street. The local reporter
investigated and made the following notes:

Guy escaped safari park 9 am.

Made for town.

Shoppers panicked – ran screaming.

Cyclist (George Carter, aged 75) fell off bike into stream in surprise.

Two cars crashed head-on – distracted by gorilla.

Guy made for greengrocers.

Quote from owner (Mrs Delia Sharp, aged 45) – It gave me quite a
turn when I went to serve the next customer and found it was a
huge gorilla! Guy seemed friendly enough, but kept banging his
chest in an alarming manner. I didn't know what to do, so
I gave him a bunch of bananas, and rang for help.

Safari ranger Tom Ball soon on scene. Guy lured into van by promise
of more bananas.

Guy back in park, unharmed by shocking (shopping) experience!

Write these notes up as a newspaper report on another sheet of paper.
Use your imagination and add more details if necessary.

GOING BANANAS!

Focus on Comprehension Teacher's Book 'C'   Text © Louis Fidge 1999   Illustrations © Nelson 1999   Published by Thomas Nelson and Sons Ltd

FURTHER TEACHING OPPORTUNITIES

Text level

Reading comprehension

▶ Before reading the story ask children to explain their idea of a hurricane, and what some of the dangers are.

▶ Ask children what impression they have of Gustus. What evidence in the text is there to support their impression of him? Why was he so determined to get to his house? What was his relationship with his Dad?

▶ Ask children to describe some of the hazards Gustus faced and overcame on the way home.

▶ The author uses some wonderfully descriptive language. Spend time studying and discussing it.

Writing composition

▶ Ask children to write the story from the father's point of view.

Sentence level

Grammatical awareness

▶ Search for, identify and classify a range of prepositions in the story. Experiment with substituting different prepositions and discuss their effect on meaning.

Sentence construction and punctuation

▶ Use the passage to study clauses. (A clause is a distinct part of a sentence including a verb.) Identify sentences with more than one clause in them. Do any of the sentences have one clause that is more important than the others (a main clause)?

Word level

Spelling

▶ Ask children to draw a chart headed one-, two-, three- and four-syllable words. Look through the text and find examples of each. Use the words for practising syllabification, identifying syllable boundaries and unstressed syllables.

Vocabulary extension

▶ Select some of the more difficult words from the text and ask children to write definitions for them, using a dictionary if necessary.

ANSWERS

Thinking back

Gustus was sheltering in the schoolhouse because of the hurricane.

He was worried about his banana tree so he set off home to check it.

As he walked the wind was raging and blowing stuff everywhere.

The river was flooded.

The bridge was nearly cracking under the strain.

The bridge gave way and Gustus was thrown into the water.

Gustus was in a daze when he reached his house.

To his surprise he found his banana tree was still standing.

Thinking about it

1 Imogene is probably the mother or sister of Gustus.

2 (open answer)   3 (open answer)

4 Lots of things would be blowing around. You could be hit by something or be carried away by the strong winds.

5 (open answer)   6 (open answer)

7 Gustus was surrounded by floating leaves, coconut husks, dead ratbats and all manner of feathered creatures and refuse.

8 (open answer)

9 His house had collapsed like an open umbrella that had been given a heavy blow.

10 Gustus hugged his tree because it meant a lot to him, and he didn't expect to find it still standing.

Thinking it through

1 (open answer)   2 (open answer)

3 (open answer)   4 (open answer)

5 (open answer)

6 There are many clues in the text. The setting of the story (coconut and banana trees, ratbats and so on) are all to be found in Jamaica. Hurricanes are also common in the Caribbean. The way the people speak in the story is also a clue.

� ➤ *Copymaster* **Book Review**

This book review pro-forma may be used to help children give their personal responses to the passage in the unit, or to any other reading book.

 # Book Review

Name _____ *Date* _____

_____

Book title _____

Author _____ Publisher _____

Story type (Tick the best word or add your own.)

adventure ☐   animal ☐   folk tale ☐   historical ☐   ghost ☐ _____

Setting

Where did the story take place? _____

When did the story take place? _____

Characters

Name the main character. _____

Describe him or her. _____

_____

_____

Plot

Write two or three sentences to say what the story was about.

_____

_____

_____

Opinion

Write some things you liked or did not like about the story.

_____

_____

_____

Write some things you liked or did not like about the author's style.

_____

_____

_____

Focus on Comprehension Teacher's Book 'C'   Text © Louis Fidge 1999 Illustrations © Nelson 1999   Published by Thomas Nelson and Sons Ltd

FURTHER TEACHING OPPORTUNITIES

Text level

Reading comprehension
► After reading the poem invite the children to express their opinions about it, in terms of content, style and structure.
► Ask children how the poet creates the sense of the continuing cycle of the sea's movements.
► Ask children what clues there are that the poem was written some time ago. Explain that Henry Wadsworth Longfellow wrote many famous poems. Ask children to find other poems by him, to read, and compare.

Writing composition
► Discuss other natural cycles, such as the daily/weekly/seasonal cycles. Ask children to construct a poem about one of these cycles, using the repetitive last line technique, modelling it on the poem in the book.

Sentence level

Grammatical awareness
► Try writing the poem in the past or future tense and note what difference this makes to the verbs.

Sentence construction and punctuation
► Discuss how the poem could be divided into many shorter sentences: for example, 'The tide rises. The tide falls.' Notice how each verse is really one long sentence. How many clauses does each sentence contain? What connectives and conjunctions does the poet use to maintain cohesion?   .

Word level

Spelling
► Use the text for a 'letter pattern' hunt. Select several key letter patterns for the children to focus on, such as 'ur', 'ea', 'ar', 'oo'. Ask children to search the passage and list all examples of words that include these patterns. Classify and study the sets of words. Does the pattern always represent the same sound when the words are spoken? Ask for suggestions of other words containing these patterns.

Vocabulary extension
► Find words in the poems that have alternative homophones: for example, tide, tied. Ask children to write the pairs of words and to make up sentences showing the differences in meaning.

ANSWERS

Thinking back
1 at twilight; 2 damp and brown; 3 the town
4 on roofs and walls; 5 soft white hands

Thinking about it
1 Twilight is when it begins to get dark in the evening.
2 A curlew is a kind of bird.
3 You can tell the traveller is in a hurry because it says he 'hastens'.
4 (open answer)
5 'The waves efface the footprints on the sand' means that the waves wash away the footprints in the sand.
6 The other name used for horses is 'steeds'.
7 A hostler was someone who looked after travellers' horses in the stables.

Thinking it through
1 The first verse is about the evening. The second verse is about the night. The third verse is about the morning. The verses show the passing of time.
2 Clues that show the poem was written some time ago include; the fact that people were using horses to travel and the use of some old-fashioned words such as hostler.
3 (open answer)   4 (open answer)

⮕ *Copymaster* **The Listeners**
Another 'classic' poem, this time by Walter de la Mare, is provided to contrast with the poem in the unit.

The Listeners

Name _____   Date _____

'Is there anybody there?' said the Traveller
Knocking on the moonlit door;
And his horse in the silence champed the grasses
Of the forest's ferny floor;
And a bird flew up out of the turret,
Above the Traveller's head.
And he smote on the door a second time;
'Is anybody there?' he said.
But no-one descended to the Traveller;
No head from the leaf-fringed sill
Leaned over and looked into his grey eyes,
Where he stood, perplexed and still.
But only a host of phantom listeners
That dwelt in the lone house then
Stood listening in the quiet of the moonlight
To that voice from the world of men;
Stood thronging the faint moonbeams on the dark stair,
That goes down to the empty hall,
Hearkening in an air stirred and shaken
By the lonely Traveller's call.
And he felt in his heart their strangeness,
Their stillness answering his cry,
While his horse moved, cropping the dark turf,
'Neath the starred and leafy sky;
For he suddenly smote on the door even
Louder, and lifted his head:
'Tell them I came and no-one answered,
That I kept my word,' he said.
Never the least stir made the listeners,
Though every word he spake
Fell echoing through the shadowiness of the still house
From the one man left awake:
Ay, they heard his foot upon the stirrup,
And the sound of iron on stone,
And how the silence surged softly backward,
When the plunging hooves were gone.

Walter de la Mare

FURTHER TEACHING OPPORTUNITIES

Text level

Reading comprehension
▶ Ask children from whose point of view the story is being told. What sort of picture is painted of Arthur?
▶ Ask children to create character profiles for Merlyn and Lady Nemue.
▶ Ask children how the author manages to create a sense of magic and mystery in the passage.
▶ Brainstorm, and list on the board, the sorts of characters, settings and events the children associate with legends of the past.
▶ Legends such as King Arthur may be considered as part of our 'literary heritage'. Ask children what they understand by this.

Writing composition
▶ Ask children to make up their own 'King Arthur' adventure, in the same style of the story.

Sentence level

Grammatical awareness
▶ Use the dialogue in the passage for reviewing work on the use of direct speech and accompanying punctuation conventions. Try translating some of the dialogue into indirect, or reported, speech.

Sentence construction and punctuation
▶ Use the passage to investigate clauses through: identifying the main clause in a long sentence; investigating sentences with more than one clause; understanding how clauses are connected (for example, by combining two or three short sentences into one).

Word level

Spelling
▶ Use the word 'encrusted' as a means to focus on prefixes. Ask children to find other words prefixed by 'en', such as encourage, enable, and to use dictionaries to find, and make lists of, words beginning with the following prefixes: 'in', 'im', 'ir', 'il', 'pro', 'sus'.

Vocabulary extension
▶ Ask children to find and write down words from the text that are difficult to understand, and to use a dictionary to help define them.

ANSWERS

Thinking back
1 a lake; 2 a sword; 3 Lady Nemue; 4 old lovers;
5 a boat; 6 jewels and gold; 7 had vanished;
8 keep him safe

Thinking about it
1 People who lived on Avalon were not living but not dead. They lived in a half-life. They had earthly and unearthly powers for good and evil.
2 (open answer)
3 The illustration shows that Merlyn was old
4 Arthur was amazed.
5 (open answer)
6 (open answer)
7 A scabbard is a holder for a sword.
8 Excalibur would bring Arthur victory and glory and honour.
9 (open answer)
10 Bercelet is probably Arthur's dog, because it says that he came up and shook himself, showering Arthur from head to toe.

Thinking it through
1 a) Arthur is telling the story. b) He is High King of Britain.
2 (open answer)
3 (open answer)
4 (open answer)

▷ *Copymaster* Oral story-telling
This copymaster provides a useful checklist in the form of a flow diagram, outlining the steps needed to memorise and present a story orally. It may be used in conjunction with the passage in the unit, or any other.

⇨➤ Oral story-telling

Name _____   Date _____

Use the story in Unit 20 to practise telling stories from memory. Here are some steps to help you:

Get the story outline clear.

Draw a few pictures or make very brief notes of key points to help you remember.

↓

Practise

Practise telling your story until you know it well.
Try it out with a partner.
Discuss your performance and consider ways of changing or improving it if necessary.

↓

Presentation

Think about presentation.
Decide whether to:
• sit or stand,
• use actions,
• use different voices for different characters.

↓

Performance

You should be ready now to tell your story to an audience.

Focus on Comprehension Teacher's Book 'C'   Text © Louis Fidge 1999 Illustrations © Nelson 1999   Published by Thomas Nelson and Sons Ltd

FURTHER TEACHING OPPORTUNITIES

Text level

Reading comprehension
▶ Discuss the effectiveness of the opening paragraph. Does it make the reader want to read on? Why?
▶ Ask children to map out, in note form, the bones of the story.
▶ Ask children to say whether they thought it was a good place to finish the extract and to justify their opinions.
▶ Ask children how the author built up the tension and a sense of expectancy throughout the passage.
▶ Ask children to express their views on the passage as a whole: the characterisation, the plot, the author's style.

Writing composition
▶ Children could be asked to continue the story in the same style as the author.
▶ The passage could be translated into a play script, using the appropriate conventions of layout, use of a narrator, scene setting, notes to actors on what they should be doing and how they should be speaking.

Sentence level

Grammatical awareness
▶ Try telling the story from one of the character's point of view, expressing it in the first person. Discuss the changes this would require.

Sentence construction and punctuation
▶ Revise the use of apostrophes, for contractions and possession, using examples from the story as a starting point.

Word level

Spelling
▶ Have a 'silent letter' word hunt. Ask children to search through the text and note down words which contain examples of a silent 'k', 's', 't', 'b'. Invite children to suggest other words with these, and other silent letters.

Vocabulary extension
▶ Find words in the story that can have a dual meaning, for example pike, left, lying. Ask children to write sentences showing the words' different meanings. Discuss whether the words are used in the same way in both sentences: are they used as nouns, verbs or whatever.

ANSWERS

Thinking back
1 The boat belonged to John, Susan, Titty and Roger.
2 A long arrow with a green feather struck the saucepan.
3 Titty did not want Roger to touch the arrow because it might be poisoned.
4 They thought it came from the owner of the boat called 'Amazon'.
5 They heard a sharp crack of a dead stick breaking, coming from the middle of the island.
6 John discovered that Swallow had gone.
7 The signal to advance was the sound of the mate blowing her whistle.
8 Roger and Titty carried a stick each.
9 Roger found a round place where the grass and ferns were pressed flat.
10 Roger discovered a knife in the grass.

Thinking about it
1 (open answer)   2 (open answer)
3 John is the leader of the group because he is called captain.
4 (open answer)   5 (open answer)
6 They kept in touch with each other by signalling.
7 (open answer)   8 (open answer)

Thinking it through
1 (open answer)
2 (open answer)
3 (open answer)
4 (open answer)
5 (open answer)

▷ *Copymaster* **Sequencing**
Children are asked to cut out and sequence correctly the main events of the passage.

 # Sequencing

Name _____   Date _____

Cut out these sentences.
Arrange them so they tell the main events of the story in order.

✂ ---

The four children kept in touch with each other by using various signals.

They saw no-one but heard the sound of a dead stick, cracking in the middle of the island.

They also found a big clasp knife which had been dropped.

John discovered that their boat, Swallow, had disappeared.

The children were round the camp-fire cooking. Suddenly they were surprised when someone fired an arrow which hit their saucepan.

Roger and Titty searched the middle of the island.

Just as John was bending down to examine the grass, there was a wild yell. Roger and Titty found a place in the grass where someone had been lying.

John ordered them to spread out and search. After Titty hooted three times, the captain and the mate appeared.

Focus on Comprehension Teacher's Book 'C'   Text © Louis Fidge 1999 Illustrations © Nelson 1999   Published by Thomas Nelson and Sons Ltd

FURTHER TEACHING OPPORTUNITIES

Text level

Reading comprehension

▶ Before reading the passage, ask if any children have read *Tom's Midnight Garden* or seen the film or TV adaptation of it. Ask them to recount their versions of the theme of the story. After reading the passage, identify similarities and differences, and discuss how reading, rather than seeing, encourages the use of the imagination more.

▶ Ask children what clues there are in the passage that the events took place in a different period.

▶ Ask children how it would feel to be Mary, in a strange house, at night, hearing sounds of crying.

▶ Ask children to suggest who the boy might be, why he is there and what might happen next.

▶ Ask children to see Mary from the boy's point of view. What thoughts and feeling would he have?

▶ In what way does this story have some similarity with the poem 'The Hairy Toe' (in Unit 3)?

Writing composition

▶ Ask children to imagine that Mary wrote to a friend about her experiences at the strange house. Invite children to write a letter, describing the house and the discovery of the boy.

Sentence level

Grammatical awareness

▶ Use the passage as an opportunity to revise work on different classes of words (parts of speech). Select one (such as prepositions) and ask children to identify all examples they can find in the text, and to explain the function they serve.

Sentence construction and punctuation

▶ Have a 'punctuation spotting' competition. See who can locate and identify the most types of punctuation mark in the passage.

Word level

Spelling

▶ Use the word 'ancient' from the text to show that the rule 'i' before 'e' except after 'c' when the sound is 'ee' doesn't always work! Brainstorm and list other examples suggested by children (quiet, science, weird, seize, protein).

Vocabulary extension

▶ Mary 'took the bull by the horns'. She boldly faced dangers and the unknown. Ask children to suggest other well-known idioms or proverbs (or supply them with some) and invite them to explain what they might mean, and to volunteer situations in which these sayings might be used.

ANSWERS

Thinking back

1 True	2 False	3 False	4 True
5 False	6 False	7 True	

Thinking about it

1 (open answer)

2 (open answer)

3 The corridor was very dark.

4 Mary could see a glimmer of light coming from the room and could hear someone crying.

5 The boy's bedroom was big, with ancient, handsome furniture in it. There was a low fire glowing faintly on the hearth and a night-light burning by the side of a carved four-poster bed hung with brocade.

6 The boy had a sharp delicate face, the colour of ivory, and he seemed to have eyes too big for it. He also had a lot of hair which tumbled over his forehead in heavy locks and made his thin face seem even smaller. He looked like a boy who had been ill.

7 The boy was surprised to see Mary. He stared at her with his eyes opened wide. He spoke in a half-frightened whisper and asked her if she was a ghost.

Thinking it through

1 (open answer)	2 (open answer)
3 (open answer)	4 (open answer)
5 (open answer)	

⇨ *Copymaster* **Being Ill**
This copymaster encourages children to empathise with the boy who is ill in the passage and relate the situation to their own personal experiences.

Name _____   *Date* _____

What do you think is wrong with this girl? Why?

_____

Describe how she might be feeling.

_____

When was the last time you were ill? What was the matter?

_____

What helped you get better?

_____

How do you pass the time when you are in bed ill?

_____

What sort of things do you miss most when you are ill?

_____

What do you think was the matter with the boy in the story in Unit 22?

_____

Why do you think Mary wasn't told about him?

_____

How will Mary help him? What will she do?
One another sheet of paper, write a paragraph on what you think happens next.

_____

Book 3 / Copymaster / Unit 22

Focus on Comprehension Teacher's Book 'C'   Text © Louis Fidge 1999 Illustrations © Nelson 1999   Published by Thomas Nelson and Sons Ltd

FURTHER TEACHING OPPORTUNITIES

Text level

Reading comprehension
► Discuss how it is possible to infer that this report came from a newspaper: for example, columns of text, style, credits at the foot.
► Explain the difference between biography and autobiography.
► Discuss some of the features of the text and encourage children to find examples of: an introduction which orientates the reader; plenty of factual details; fairly objective, impersonal style; written in the third person; structured into paragraphs, each with a different main idea.

Writing composition
► Ask children to write a biographical account of what they can discover of Long Wolf from the text.

Sentence level

Grammatical awareness
► Use the passage as a basis for reviewing work on nouns. Read through the text and identify all the nouns. Ask children to say whether they are singular or plural, common, proper, abstract or collective. Ask them to explain the different characteristics of each type of noun.

Sentence construction and punctuation
► Select sentences from the text which contain examples of connectives being used to help structure the sentence. For example '*When* the Sioux were finally overcome, *however*, he …' Ask children to identify the linking connectives.

Word level

Spelling
► Ask children to find and list examples of words which have been prefixed in some way, such as repatriated. Discuss what effect the prefix has on the root word's meaning. Study other prefixes such as 'bi', 'con', 'in', 'prim', 'sub', 'tele'.

Vocabulary extension
► Discuss how native Americans' names were all relevant to their culture and life-style. Ask

children to think up other names which might have been given to native Americans. This could lead in to a study of children's forenames (what they mean and why they were called them) and surnames, especially their links with occupations (for example, Smith, Thatcher, Archer).

ANSWERS

Thinking back
1 Long Wolf was a Sioux Indian Chief.
2 He came with 'Buffalo Bill' Cody's Wild West Show.
3 He died of pneumonia in 1892.
4 He was buried at Brompton Cemetery in London.
5 His dying wish was to be returned to America.
6 Jessie Black Feather, Long Wolf's grand-daughter, came to take him home.
7 He will be buried at Pine Ridge Reservation in Wounded Knee.
8 Elizabeth Knight found his grave and contacted his descendants.

Thinking about it
1 The Sioux were an Indian tribe in America.
2 It says he 'When the Sioux were finally overcome'.
3 (open answer)
4 (open answer)
5 (open answer)
6 He couldn't believe it. He felt excited.
7 (open answer)

Thinking it through
1 (open answer)   2 (open answer)
3 a) neglected: not looked after
  b) descendants: people who have a particular person as an ancestor
  c) exhumed: dug up
  d) repatriation: sending or bringing a person back to his own country
4 (open answer)   5 (open answer)

⇨ *Copymaster* **Making Notes**
This copymaster helps develop the skill of making notes by underlining key words, and is based on parts of the text from the unit.

Making Notes

Name _____   Date _____

When we make notes we only need to note key words and phrases.

Chief <u>Long Wolf fought with</u> the <u>Sioux against</u> the <u>US army</u> and,
according to his family, <u>helped</u> to <u>defeat</u> General <u>Custer</u> at <u>Little
Big Horn</u> in <u>1876</u>. When the Sioux were finally overcome,
however, he <u>joined 'Buffalo Bill' Cody's Wild West Show</u>. In <u>1892</u>
he <u>contracted pneumonia</u> on a trip to <u>London</u> to perform at
Earls Court, <u>died</u>, and was <u>buried</u> by Cody at <u>Brompton
Cemetery</u>, where his <u>grave</u> has lain <u>untended for decades</u>.

The notes are much shorter:
Long Wolf fought with Sioux against US army – helped defeat
Custer, Little Big Horn 1876 – joined 'Buffalo Bill' Cody's Wild
West Show – 1892 contracted pneumonia – London – died –
buried Brompton Cemetery – grave untended for decades

Underline the key words in this:

Yesterday, Jessie Black Feather, 87, the grand-daughter and oldest
descendant of Long Wolf, said: 'We have come to England to fulfil
my grandfather's dying wish to be returned to America.' Jessie's
mother, Lizzie, was 12 and with her father in London when he
died. The family was unable to take his body home immediately,
and after she returned to America she lost track of where Long
Wolf was buried. His body will be exhumed on Thursday, taken
in a horse-drawn carriage to the gates of the cemetery, then
flown home. He will be buried on Sunday with Indian and
Christian ceremonies at the ancestral burial ground of the Ogala
Sioux tribe at Pine Ridge Reservation in Wounded Knee.

On another sheet of paper, write some short notes about the paragraph above.

FURTHER TEACHING OPPORTUNITIES

Text level

Reading comprehension

▶ Before reading the poem, help set it briefly in context by explaining some of the tensions and conflicts between the native American peoples and the needs of the settlers and pioneers as they expanded their horizons and looked for 'pastures new'.

▶ Ask children to find examples in the poem which show that the native Americans lived in harmony with nature.

▶ Discuss the rich figurative language used in the poem.

▶ Ask children if this poem could be considered as a piece of 'persuasive' writing. If so, how?

▶ Ask children if they think parts of our world are 'alive'? Why shouldn't we use nature as we please?

Writing composition

▶ Ask children to think of five good reasons why we should look after our planet and conserve its resources. Then ask them to make this into an attractive poster to remind people.

Sentence level

Grammatical awareness

▶ Use the poem as a way of revising pronouns. Identify all the pronouns in it and ask children to say who, or what, each stands for. Consider whether the pronouns are personal or possessive, first, second or third person, singular or plural.

Sentence construction and punctuation

▶ The poem contains a variety of punctuation marks: commas, full stops, question marks, hyphens, colons, apostrophes (marking contractions and possessions). Read the poem again, noting the function of each punctuation mark, and how important they are to the reader.

Word level

Spelling

▶ Ask the children to find at least one example of words containing the following common word endings: 'ible', 'ive', 'ment', 'or', 'tion', 'ness', 'ious', 'igh'. Brainstorm other words with the same endings and list them for spelling practice.

Vocabulary extension

▶ Select a number of words beginning with a particular letter from the text, such as 'm'. Ask children to arrange these in alphabetical order and write definitions for them.

ANSWERS

Thinking back

1 Chief Seattle spoke the words of the poem in 1855.

2 He was speaking to the US Government.

3 He spoke to them because they wanted to buy the lands of his native American people.

4 The reasons could include: because they are the blood of your grandfather's grandfather; they quench our thirst; they carry our canoes; they feed our children.

5 His grandfather said the air is precious.

Thinking about it

1 (open answer)   2 (open answer)
3 (open answer)   4 (open answer)
5 (open answer)

Thinking it through

1 (open answer)   2 (open answer)
3 (open answer)   4 (open answer)

➡ Copymaster   The Peace Pipe

The copymaster contains an extract from Longfellow's 'Hiawatha'. This provides an opportunity to compare and contrast two pieces both with the linking theme of native Americans.

The Peace Pipe

Name _____   *Date* _____

Gitche Manito, the mighty,
The creator of the nations,
Looked upon them with compassion,
With paternal love and pity;
Looked upon their wrath and
    wrangling
But as quarrels among children,
But as feuds and fights of children!

Over them he stretched his right hand,
To subdue their stubborn natures,
To allay their thirsts and fever,
By the shadow of his right hand;
Spake to them with voice majestic,
As the sound of far-off waters
Falling into deep abysses,
Warning, chiding, spake in this wise:

'O my children! my poor children!
Listen to the words of wisdom,
Listen to the words of warning,
From the lips of the Great Spirit,
From the Master of Life who made
    you!
I have given you lands to hunt in,
I have given you lands to fish in,
I have given you bear and bison,
I have given you roe and reindeer,
I have given you brant and beaver,
Filled the marshes full of wild-fowl,
Filled the rivers full of fishes;
Why then are you not contented?
Why then will you hunt each other?

I am weary of your quarrels,
Weary of your wars and bloodshed,
Weary of your prayers for vengeance,
Of your wranglings and dissensions;
All your strength is in your union,
All your danger is in discord;
Therefore be at peace hence forward,
And as brothers live together.'

Henry Wadsworth Longfellow (from 'Hiawatha')

Focus on Comprehension Teacher's Book 'C'   Text © Louis Fidge 1999   Illustrations © Nelson 1999   Published by Thomas Nelson and Sons Ltd

FURTHER TEACHING OPPORTUNITIES

Text level

Reading comprehension

▶ Discuss the children's responses to the text after reading it. How did the writer make them feel?

▶ What did the children think of the author's style? Explore how she manages to generate a sense of menace.

▶ From whose point of view is the story told? Ask children to suggest how the Headmaster might have seen the episode.

Writing composition

▶ Ask children to imagine, and write about, meeting someone who makes them feel uncomfortable (like the Headmaster). Ask them to consider a) the setting (where they meet the person) b) their actions (what they do and say) c) their appearance (how they look).

Sentence level

Grammatical awareness

▶ Use the passage to revise work on adjectives. Ask children to write down all the adjectives they can find. Try substituting different adjectives. How does this affect the meaning?

Sentence construction and punctuation

▶ Find simple conjunctions (such as 'and', 'but') in the passage which serve to join shorter sentences into longer sentences. Ask children to try breaking down the longer sentences and writing them as a series of shorter ones.

▶ Note the use of connectives (words and phrases) that help sequence the text: such as, 'until', 'as'.

Word level

Spelling

▶ Identify and list a given number of polysyllabic words from the text. Say them and work out how many syllables each consists of. Remind children that, where there is a double consonant, the syllable boundary falls between the consonants: for example, fol - low - ing. Practise syllabifying the polysyllabic words and marking in syllable boundaries. Refer to dictionaries to see how this is shown in them. Consider which of the syllables are stressed and unstressed in the words.

Vocabulary extension

▶ Use the saying on the notice as a way of focusing on proverbs. Provide the children with some well-known proverbs, such as 'Empty vessels make most noise', and ask them to explain what they mean and how they might have originated. Ask children to suggest others they know.

ANSWERS

Thinking back

1 The girl's name was Dinah.
2 Jeff took her to see the Headmaster.
3 The corridor walls were bare.
4 The man who can keep order can rule the world.
5 It was the tidiest office she had ever seen. There were no papers, no files, no pictures on the walls. Just a large empty-topped desk, a filing cabinet and a bookcase with a neat row of books.
6 He was tall and thin, dressed in an immaculate black suit. From his shoulders, a long, black teacher's gown hung in heavy folds, like wings. Only his head was startlingly white. His eyes were hidden behind dark glasses, like two black holes in the middle of the whiteness.

Thinking about it

1 (open answer)   2 (open answer)
3 (open answer)
4 His long black teacher's gown, with heavy folds like wings, gave him the appearance of a crow.
5 a) (open answer)   b) (open answer)

Thinking it through

1 a) (open answer)   b) (open answer)
   c) (open answer)
2 (open answer)
3 a) (open answer)   b) (open answer)
   c) (open answer)

⇨ *Copymaster* Facing Fear
This traditional story is also about facing fear. It is in the form of a cloze procedure.

➡ Facing Fear

Name _____   Date _____

**Think of a suitable word to fill each gap
in this story from Sudan.**

The king was getting too _____ to fight, so when the Moors

_____ to attack, he asked his _____, Prince Sana, to _____

the army. Prince Sana was big and brave-looking, but his heart was full

of _____. His _____, the Princess, had an idea. 'I will wear

your armour and everyone will think I am _____!' she said. The

_____ put on his _____ and rode out _____ his big

white stallion.

    That _____ day, the Moors launched a fierce _____. The

Princess led the army _____, and _____ them back. They

attacked _____, but once more they were _____ back. After

a while, _____ of the soldiers began to _____ that the

person who was leading them was not _____ the Prince. The

horse was his. The armour was his. But the person in _____

seemed to be much _____ than the Prince. _____ began to

spread. The Princess knew what to do. _____ told the Prince to

put on _____ armour and go and show _____ to his men.

She rode with him so the _____ could see them both together.

As they _____ into view the Princess whipped Sana's _____

and made it bolt forward. Try as he might, the _____ could not

stop the horse. To his _____, he saw that he was galloping

_____ the enemy camp! When the lookouts saw the Prince on

his _____ horse coming straight towards them, they fell into a

_____. The Prince took out his _____ and waved it in the

air. The enemy _____ fled in terror.

Focus on Comprehension Teacher's Book 'C'   Text © Louis Fidge 1999 Illustrations © Nelson 1999   Published by Thomas Nelson and Sons Ltd

FURTHER TEACHING OPPORTUNITIES

Text level

Reading comprehension

▶ Stories about Nasreddin Hodja abound in the Middle East. They are usually about everyday events and make us think about life and people's behaviour. Discuss how this is true of this story.

▶ Ask children what clues there are that this story comes from another culture.

▶ Ask children in what sense the Hodja is 'as stubborn as a mule'.

Writing composition

▶ Ask children to try writing the story from a particular person's perspective, such as the wife's or the boy's.

Sentence level

Grammatical awareness

▶ Transform some of the sentences in the passage from the active into the passive form. For example, 'A thief broke into the Hodja's house' would become 'The Hodja's house was broken into by a thief.' Note and discuss how changes from the active to passive affect the word order and sense of a sentence.

Sentence construction and punctuation

▶ Ask children to find examples of connectives (words and phrases) in the story, which mark the passing of time: for example 'one day', 'in the meantime', 'then'.

Word level

Spelling

▶ Find words in the text containing 'ie'. Remind children of the rule 'i' before 'e' except after 'c' when it says 'ee'. Do the 'ie' words in the text follow that rule? Ask children to suggest as many 'ie' words as possible. Does the word 'neighbour' follow this rule? Think of other words in which the 'ei' is pronounced 'ay'.

Vocabulary extension

▶ There are many expressions containing references to animals: for example, 'she goes like a bird', 'let the cat out of the bag', 'let sleeping dogs lie', 'don't count your chickens until they're hatched', 'birds of a feather flock together', 'to take the bull by the horns', 'to smell a rat'. Ask children to suggest others and what they mean.

ANSWERS

Thinking back
1 <u>feeding his donkey</u>.
2 <u>the Hodja's job</u>.
3 <u>some soup</u>.
4 <u>kavuk (hat)</u>.
5 <u>on the Hodja's head</u>.
6 <u>hurried home</u>.
7 <u>he had won</u>.
8 <u>obstinate</u>.

Thinking about it
1 Answers could include: he had a donkey; he was married; he was a scholar; he wore a kavuk; he was stubborn.
2 a) Answers could include: she was married to the Hodja; she thought the Hodja was stubborn; she did not want to feed the donkey; she had a friend nearby.
   b) Answers could include: she lived near the Hodja; she was friendly with his wife; she had a son; she was kind.
   c) Answers could include: he robbed the Hodja's house; he stole all the valuables; he even stole the Hodja's kavuk.
3 (open answer)
4 (open answer)
5 He rejoiced because it meant he had won.

Thinking it through
1 (open answer)   2 (open answer)
3 (open answer)   4 (open answer)
5 (open answer)

⇨▶ *Copymaster*
The Kind Man and the Robber
The children are asked to sequence a set of sentences in order to re-tell a traditional Iraqi story.

The Kind Man and the Robber

Name _____   Date _____

Cut out these sentences and arrange them in order to tell a traditional story from Iraq.

Just as he was about to leave he heard someone come in the front door.

The old man asked the robber if he would like some help to carry the bundles.

Off they set, but after a little while the old man became tired and began to stumble with his bundle of cloth.

The robber was astonished that anyone could be so kind.

One night in Baghdad a robber broke into a house and stole many bundles of fine cloth.

He felt so ashamed that he broke down in tears, and asked the old man to forgive him.

The old man said that the cloth was all his anyway because it was his house that the robber had broken into! He told the robber that he was happy for him to have his cloth if he really needed it.

The old man willingly forgave him – and the robber promised to try to live a better life after that.

When he looked up he saw it was a weak old man.

The robber shouted angrily at him and said that if they did not reach his house by sunrise they would get caught.

When they reached the robber's house he told the old man to take a little of the cloth and clear off.

Book 4 / Copymaster / Unit 4

Focus on Comprehension Teacher's Book 'C'   Text © Louis Fidge 1999   Illustrations © Nelson 1999   Published by Thomas Nelson and Sons Ltd

FURTHER TEACHING OPPORTUNITIES

Text level

Reading comprehension
- ▶ Ask children to explain how they know this is a piece of autobiographical writing.
- ▶ Ask children how well Ahmed gave an account of the sort of life he leads. Did children feel they knew him better by the end of the article?
- ▶ Ask children if, by and large, Ahmed enjoys his work. Find evidence to support answers.
- ▶ In a part of the article not reproduced, Ahmed says 'I'm sad because I know none of my sons will become a shepherd like me.' Ask children to suggest why he thinks this.

Writing composition
- ▶ Use the article as a basis for writing a similar brief article by Ahmed in the same style, suggesting that being a shepherd is a) a lonely life b) not a lonely life c) a hard life d) an easy life.

Sentence level

Grammatical awareness
- ▶ Ask children to try writing some of the account in the third person, rather than the first person, and noting what changes are required.
- ▶ Rewrite some of the sentences incorrectly on the board, introducing a lack of agreement between subjects and verb: for example, 'Then I feeds the flocks.' Ask children to rewrite them correctly, explaining why they were incorrect.

Sentence construction and punctuation
- ▶ Select some complex sentences and ask children to rewrite them in a simpler form, making any additions or changes necessary to do so. For example, 'As soon as I wake up, before sunrise, I open the gate for the goats and sheep and tell them to go out on the hillside' could be written, 'I wake up before sunrise. My first job is to ...'.

Word level

Spelling
- ▶ Ask children to find a given number of words in the text that have been suffixed in some way: for example 'centuries'. Identify and write the root word for each to explain how the suffix has affected its meaning and its spelling.

Vocabulary extension
- ▶ Our language is full of words we have 'borrowed' from other languages such as 'bazaar', 'caravan', borrowed from the Middle East. Ask children to check the meaning and etymology of these words in a dictionary.

ANSWERS

Thinking back
1 <u>Bethlehem</u>; 2 <u>father</u>; 3 <u>seven</u>; 4 <u>goats</u>; 5 <u>name</u>; 6 <u>steel</u>; 7 <u>rains</u>; 8 <u>graze</u>; 9 <u>enclosure (fenced off area)</u>; 10 <u>grains</u>.

Thinking about it
1 (open answer)
2 (open answer)
3 He gives them extra grain because there is not enough grass for them to eat.
4 The main dangers to the sheep are being hunted by wild animals or being stolen by robbers.
5 (open answer)
6 First he milks the sheep, then cleans and purifies the milk and stirs it. When the milk has turned into cheese he covers it with white paper and presses it until all the water is removed. He adds salt and places the cheese into bags.

Thinking it through
1 (open answer)
2 (open answer)
3 (open answer)
4 a) turbulent: restless and noisy
   b) enclosure: land surrounded by a fence
   c) graze: to feed on growing grass
   d) vegetation: plant life
   e) sparse: scarce
   f) barren: unable to produce vegetation
   g) predators: animals that hunt others
5 (open answer)

⇨ *Copymaster* **Shepherds**
This copymaster asks children to think further about the life of Ahmed (from the text in the unit), and to compare aspects of their lives with his.

⇨ Shepherds

Name _____   *Date* _____

**Write some things you already knew about
shepherds before you read the text.**

_____

_____

_____

**Write the thing you found most interesting
about the life of Ahmed Abyyiat, the shepherd.**

_____

_____

_____

What other interesting facts did you discover?

_____

_____

Write some of the skills you think a shepherd needs.

_____

_____

Compare some aspects of your life with Ahmed's.

	Ahmed	Me
Number in family		
Place to live		
Place to sleep		
Time of getting up		
Clothes worn		
Favourite food		
What occupies most days		
What occupies most evenings		

FURTHER TEACHING OPPORTUNITIES

Text level

Reading comprehension
▶ How well does this passage conform to the 'ghost story' genre in terms of characters, settings, plot and so on? How does the end of the text begin to undermine or explain the 'supernatural'?
▶ Ask the children in what sense did the two boys' 'curiosity get the better of them'.
▶ Discuss how the author's use of words engender a 'spooky' feeling.
▶ Encourage the children to articulate their personal responses to the text, identifying how and why the text affects them.

Writing composition
▶ Ask children to write a 'ghost' story in the same vein. They should try to use the flashback technique in which the story begins with a dramatic section, the part which might normally have been the climax of the story ('In rushed a bony figure, with wild white hair, and a face like a skeleton, screaming and shaking') and then retrace the steps building up to it.

Sentence level

Grammatical awareness
▶ Identify the prepositions in the passage and comment on their function. Experiment with substituting different prepositions and discuss the difference this makes to meaning. Note occasions where verb and preposition come together, as in 'came from'.

Sentence construction and punctuation
▶ Try rewriting some complex sentences by moving the position of clauses about within the sentences.

Word level

Spelling
▶ Find words in the text that make the sound 'air', such as 'hair', 'there', 'their' 'dare'. Ask children to think of other words with these letter patterns.
▶ Have other 'letter pattern hunts' based on the text. Supply patterns for children to look for, such as 'oo', 'ow', 'ea'. Are these always pronounced the same? Build up word lists based on these for spelling practice.

Vocabulary extension
▶ Search for words in the text that could be spelt in a different way yet still sound the same (homonyms), such as pane/pain. Ask children to compose pairs of sentences, using the words to show that they understand their meanings.

ANSWERS

Thinking back
1 Jim and Arthur heard screams coming from the house.
2 They always ran away when they heard the screams.
3 Arthur thought there was a witch in the house.
4 One day the two boys saw a girl at one of the windows.
5 Jim went in to find the girl and left Arthur outside.
6 The boys dived under a dust sheet.
7 Mary sat her Gran in a chair and stopped her screaming.
8 Mary explained that her Gran was having a 'turn'.

Thinking about it
1 (open answer)
2 Jim is older because the text says 'Little Arthur', and says that Jim is bigger than Arthur.
3 (open answer) 4 (open answer)
5 a) Mary was fair-haired and a little skinny.
  b) Mary's Gran was bony, dressed all in black with wild white hair, and stick-like arms.
6 (open answer) 7 (open answer)

Thinking it through
1 (open answer) 2 (open answer)
3 (open answer) 4 (open answer)
5 a) (open answer) b) (open answer)

⇨ *Copymaster   Detective Work*
This copymaster asks children to interrogate the text in the unit in a variety of ways and write up their conclusions in the form of a detective's report.

Detective Work

Name _____   Date _____

Write up your notes on 'It's Too Frightening for Me'.

Who? (Main characters and brief factual details of each)

What? (What happened? To whom? How?)

Where? (Location)

Why? (What caused it? Is there an explanation? What is the evidence?)

Conclusion (Suggest what might happen next.)

Signed: _____

Focus on Comprehension Teacher's Book 'C'   Text © Louis Fidge 1999 Illustrations © Nelson 1999   Published by Thomas Nelson and Sons Ltd

FURTHER TEACHING OPPORTUNITIES

Text level

Reading comprehension
▶ Get the children to practise reading and performing the poem. Discuss the importance of the rhythmic scanning and rhyming elements, and noting the poet's use of onomatopoeic sound words.
▶ Ask the children how the poet builds up tension and menace in the first three verses. Discuss how the crisis is resolved in the last verse. How well does this poem fit the literary form of introduction – build-up – crisis – resolution?

Writing composition
▶ Ask the children to make up their own poem about 'The Snyke' or 'The Doze'. Remind them to think about its appearance, where it lives, whether it is friendly or fierce, what it eats, how it moves, how it behaves and so on.

Sentence level

Grammatical awareness
▶ The writer has written sentences in a poetic form: for example 'Along the valley of the Ump gallops the fearful Hippocrump.' Ask children to rewrite some selected sentences in more conventional prose style.

Sentence construction and punctuation
▶ Punctuation marks are a critical part of a poet's armoury. Read the poem again. Ask children to identify each type of punctuation mark, and explain its importance.

Word level

Spelling
▶ Give children the following words: boat, sense, word, scene, whole, ditch, cries, round, dawn, boil, weed, pray, caught, root. For each word, ask them to try to think of rhyming words that a) have the same letter pattern b) have a different letter pattern.

Vocabulary extension
▶ List all the onomatopoeic words in the poem. Ask children to suggest as many others as possible: for example, noises engines make, street sounds, animal noises.

ANSWERS

Thinking back
1 False 2 True 3 Can't tell
4 True 5 True 6 True
7 True 8 False

Thinking about it
1 (open answer)
2 It makes the Hippocrump's teeth ache, and then makes it stamp and roar.
3 (open answer)
4 a) The cattle faint with fright, the birds fall flat, and the fish turn white.
b) The rocks begin to shake.
c) The sleeping children wake up.
d) The old people quiver, quail and quake.
5 (open answer)
6 a) The people prayed to their god to help save them.
b) A broken stump caught the Hippocrump in the rump and threw him into the river, which cured him of his fever.
c) They sang glad hymns of praise.
7 a) (open answer) b) (open answer)

Thinking it through
1 (open answer) 2 (open answer)
3 (open answer) 4 (open answer)
5 (open answer)
6 a) hideous: extremely ugly
b) falters: stumbles or walks unsteadily
c) baneful: troublesome (or poisonous)
d) resounding: loud or echoing
e) quail: lose courage or shrink back in fear
f) intruder: an unexpected or unwelcome visitor
g) flounder: to struggle awkwardly
h) serene: calm and peaceful.

⇨ *Copymaster* **The Osc**
The Osc is another imaginary animal and is a complete contrast to the Hippocrump.

Name _____   *Date* _____

This is the superfluminous Osc,
  A mild and serious liver,
He skims each day from dawn till dusk
  The surface of the river.

For gentleness he is the best
  Of all amphibious creatures;
His wide and wondering eyes suggest
  An old, forgotten teacher's.

In, out—in, out—he weaves his way
  Along the limpid shallows,
Or upside-down hangs half a day
  Amidst the ruminous sallows.

In mating time he bleats and sings
  To entertain his bride,
He wiggles both his graceful wings
  And jumps from side to side.

No hawk invades his harmless path,
  No boar with cruel tusk,
No alligator mad with wrath
  Attacks the little Osc.

He lives on fluff and water-weed
  And bits of this and that
Which other creatures do not need.
  His ears are round and flat.

Thus, free from terror, want and sin,
  Proceeds from dusk to dusk
Out, in—out, in—with careless fin
  The superfluminous Osc.

From *Prefabulous Animiles* by James Reeves

FURTHER TEACHING OPPORTUNITIES

Text level

Reading comprehension

▶ What was the overall impact of the text on the children? How successful was the writer in building up suspense, fear, terror?

▶ Ask children to decide through whose eyes this passage is told. Which sections tell the reader what Lucy was thinking and feeling? Were the children able to empathise with Lucy?

▶ What did the children think of the writer's style and use of language?

▶ If possible, read excerpts from Ted Hughes 'The Iron Man'. Compare and contrast the style and theme of both books.

Writing composition

▶ How could this story continue? Brainstorm ideas with the class. Note ideas and suggestions on the board. Encourage children to emulate the use of powerful and descriptive language and the style of the passage.

Sentence level

Grammatical awareness

▶ Study and discuss some of the dramatic descriptions and powerful figurative language of the text – the use of simile and metaphor.

Sentence construction and punctuation

▶ Encourage the children to speculate and write their own questions using conditionals, that is, words like 'if ... then', 'might', 'could', 'would'.

Word level

Spelling

▶ Find the words 'much', 'machinery', 'stomach' in the text. Discuss the different sound values of 'ch'. Build up lists of words with each sound value.

▶ Find words containing a soft 'c' or 'g' in the text, such as 'ceiling', bulged. Ask children for other similar words. Work out a rule as to when the 'c' and 'g' make a soft sound.

Vocabulary extension

▶ Find and list as many compound words (such as 'earthquake') as possible from the text.

▶ Find as many words in the text as possible that can have two meanings, such as calf, chest. Ask children to write sentences making their meanings clear, and to say what class of word (noun, verb, or whatever) the word is in each sentence.

ANSWERS

Thinking back

When the bridge shook, Lucy thought it was an earthquake.
Lucy tried to run away but she tripped over.
As she lay on the ground Lucy heard a weird sound.
First the head came out of the mud.
Next it sat upright like a gigantic dinosaur.
Then, with a groaning wail, the thing stood erect.

Thinking about it

1 Lucy thought it might be an earthquake because the ground shook and the surface of the water rippled.
2 The weird sound frightened her and made Lucy jump and run blindly.
3 The 'thing' disturbed a seagull, grass snakes and water voles.
4 The 'thing' became human-looking as it sat up.

Thinking it through

1 (open answer)   2 (open answer)
3 (open answer)
4 a) (open answer) b) (open answer)
   c) (open answer) d) (open answer)

➡ *Copymaster*   **A Letter to Lucy**
The children are asked to write a letter to Lucy, the main character in the passage in the unit, and ask her questions that are left unanswered in the text.

# A Letter to Lucy

Name _____   Date _____

Write a letter to Lucy. There must be many things you would like to say to her, and ask her, after reading Unit 8!

Dear Lucy,

I have just read an extract from the Iron Woman by Ted Hughes and I thought I would like to write to you. It must have been a terrifying experience for you – but what on earth were you doing on the marsh on your own? Don't you know how risky this is?

Yours sincerely,

Focus on Comprehension Teacher's Book 'C'   Text © Louis Fidge 1999 Illustrations © Nelson 1999   Published by Thomas Nelson and Sons Ltd

FURTHER TEACHING OPPORTUNITIES

Text level

Reading comprehension

▶ The introduction to this poem (not included in the unit) says 'A poem for children ill in bed, indicating to them the oddities of our English orthography'. Ask children to explain what they think this means.

▶ Discuss the structure of the poem: that is, it is in verses, each with four lines. The alternate lines of each verse rhyme. (Note that it is only the rhyming words that are misspelt.)

Writing composition

▶ Ask children to begin with a well-known nursery rhyme or rhyming poem and experiment with misspelling the rhyming words, using the poem as a model. Once they have got the idea, they can try making up their own poem.

Sentence level

Grammatical awareness

▶ Try rewriting the poem in continuous prose, all in the passive voice, with the class. This will mean taking some liberties with the wording and sentence structures at times! For example, the first verse might become: 'A kangaroo was kept by the professor as a pet. In March flu developed from the kangaroo's cough.'

Sentence construction and punctuation

▶ Some of the verses (for example, the first) are in fact single sentences that are very long and complicated. Discuss how the verses could be broken down into shorter, simpler sentences (written in conventional prose, not in poetry form).

Word level

Spelling

▶ Ask children to volunteer some tricky words from the extract, such as professor. Ask children for suggestions of ways in which they could remember the spellings of these words.

Vocabulary extension

▶ The month of March is named after Mars, the Roman god of war. Ask the children to research the origins of the names of the other months and days of the week. Use an etymological dictionary if possible.

ANSWERS

Thinking back

1 kangaroo; pet
2 March; cough
3 hospital
4 lemon; fleas; tapwater
5 shivered; scowled
6 laughed; jumped
7 tree

Thinking about it

1 It is more likely to be set in Australia, because that is where most kangaroos are to be found.
2 (open answer)
3 No. A kangaroo could not really be taken to hospital (unless it was an animal hospital!)
4 (open answer)
5 It made the kangaroo shiver and scowl, laugh oddly and jump out of the armchair, through the window and sit on the topmost branch of a tree.
6 It did surprise the professor. The text says that the professor was astonished.
7 (open answer)

Thinking it through

1 (open answer)   2 (open answer)
3 (open answer)
4 a) eminent: famous   b) infernal: devilish
   c) scowled: looked angrily or sullenly
   d) vaulted: leapt or jumped

⇨ *Copymaster* Hints on Pronunciation for Foreigners

This amusing poem has a similar theme to that in the unit, and draws attention to the vagaries of our spelling system.

Hints on Pronunciation to Foreigners

Name _____   *Date* _____

I take it you already know
Of tough and bough and cough and dough?
Others may stumble, but not you
On hiccough, thorough, laugh and through?
Well done! And now you wish perhaps
To learn of less familiar traps?

Beware of heard, a dreadful word
That looks like beard and sounds like bird.
And dead: it's said like bed, not bead –
For goodness sake don't call it 'deed'!
Watch out for meat and great and threat,
They rhyme with suite and straight and debt.

A moth is not a moth in mother
Nor both in bother, broth in brother,
And here is not a match for there
Nor dear and fear for bear and pear,
And then there's dose and rose and lose –
Just look them up – and goose and choose.

And cork and work and card and ward,
And font and front and word and sword,
And do and go and thwart and cart –
Come, come, I've hardly made a start!
A dreadful language? Man alive,
I'd mastered it when I was five.

Anon.

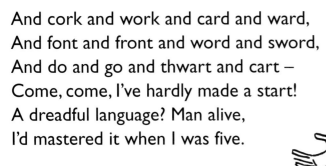

Focus on Comprehension Teacher's Book 'C'   Text © Louis Fidge 1999 Illustrations © Nelson 1999   Published by Thomas Nelson and Sons Ltd

FURTHER TEACHING OPPORTUNITIES

Text level

Reading comprehension
- ▶ Ask children what they think the purpose of the Introduction is? Point out how it orientates the reader and sets the scene, putting the achievement in perspective.
- ▶ Ask children if the text in the 'Key events' section is biographical or autobiographical. Discuss the way it is set out. In what way is the information selective? What image of the man does it set out to focus on?
- ▶ Ask children how the third section is structured. What is the purpose of the report? Why might it have been written in telegraphic note form?
- ▶ Discuss and find examples of the following features of the text: mainly factual; fairly impersonal style; written in the third person.

Writing composition
- ▶ Ask children to write an account of Webb's swim in the first person, from his point of view. Base it on the extracts from the report.

Sentence level

Grammatical awareness
- ▶ Point out that the verbs in the first section are in the present tense, whilst those in the second and third sections are in the past tense. Ask children to suggest why this is.

Sentence construction and punctuation
- ▶ Rewrite the 'Key events' section in the same telegraphic note form style as the last section. Rewrite the last section in expanded, proper sentences. Discuss which types of words are omitted or added.

Word level

Spelling
- ▶ Look at the words 'world' and 'was' from the text. How are the 'a' and 'o' pronounced? Referring to dictionaries, list other words beginning with 'wa' and 'wo'. Ask children to categorise the words according to the way the 'a' or 'o' is pronounced.

Vocabulary extension
- ▶ There are several place names in the text. Use these to discuss place name origins. Use an atlas to find place names which contain Viking words (Kes<u>wick</u>, Grims<u>by</u>). Wick (means village), beck (a brook), by (a town).

ANSWERS

Thinking back
1 Answers could include: coldness, monotony, attacks from jellyfish, drifting seaweed.
2 Matthew Webb was born in Dudley, Shropshire.
3 He learned to swim in the River Severn.
4 He rescued his younger brother from drowning.
5 He became interested in 1860.
6 He tried to rescue a sailor who had fallen overboard.
7 He was a Captain.
8 He swam on Tuesday 24 August 1875.

Thinking about it
1 (open answer)   2 (open answer)
3 Answers could include: tidal streams, drifting seaweed, being stung by a yellow star fish, change in weather.
4 a) (open answer)
  b) Webb would have been encouraged because passengers cheered him.
5 (open answer)
6 He was in the sea for about 21 hours.

Thinking it through
1 (open answer)
2 a) (open answer)   b) (open answer)
3 a) 20 breast strokes every minute.
  b) there was a strong north-easterly tidal stream which Webb had to swim against.
  c) Webb was becoming very weak and was unable to talk very well.
4 The report is written in note form and not always in proper sentences.
5 (open answer)

⇨ *Copymaster* **Biographical and Autobiographical Writing**
Children are asked to do some biographical and autobiographical writing about Matthew Webb.

⇨ **Biographical and Autobiographical Writing**

Name _____   *Date* _____

Use these notes about Matthew Webb to help you write a paragraph of autobiographical information about him.

Born 1848 – Dudley, Shropshire – 1856 rescued young brother from drowning   1860 joined naval training ship – 1873 awarded medal for rescuing drowning sailor – 1875 left merchant navy – became first man to swim Channel.

_____

_____

_____

_____

Now use the extracts from page 27 to help you to continue this biographical account of the swim as Matthew Webb might have written it.

It was a warm summer's day when I dived off Admiralty Pier at Dover, at the beginning of my attempt to be the first man to swim across the Channel to France. The date was 24th August 1875. I began swimming steadily, using the breast stroke, doing about twenty strokes to the minute.

FURTHER TEACHING OPPORTUNITIES

Text level

Reading comprehension
▶ Take the opportunity to find and discuss some of the following features of the letter:
  – impersonal, formal style of language (note way the letter opens and closes, the stilted sentence structures and vocabulary);
  – references to official organisations, laws, etc.;
  – inclusion of instructions/requests;
  – clear, unambiguous heading;
  – amount and type of detail, and formality of the layout at the top of letter before the actual letter itself even begins.

Writing composition
▶ Encourage children to compose and write three different types of letters, and to consider the degree of formality required, conventions of opening and closing letters, and layout. Compare the differences across the three letters.
Some suggestions:
  – an informal letter, such as a thank-you letter;
  – a semi-formal letter, for example a letter from the school to all parents;
  – a formal letter, such as a letter of complaint to the manufacturers of a new electrical gadget.

Sentence level

Grammatical awareness
▶ Discuss the use of the passive form in the letter (such as 'Your company has been selected').
▶ Find and discuss examples of the use of the present and future tense.

Sentence construction and punctuation
▶ Study selected sentences from the letter. Work out how many clauses each sentence contains. Note where connectives or conjunctions are used to join them together. Discuss which is the main clause in each sentence.

Word level

Spelling
▶ Identify and list polysyllabic words from the text. Say them and work out how many syllables each

consists of. Practise syllabifying the polysyllabic words and marking in syllable boundaries. Consider which of the syllables are unstressed.

Vocabulary extension
▶ Research the origins of proper names such as the names of models of cars, sportswear, newspapers. Ask children to make up some appropriate new names for products.

ANSWERS

Thinking back
1 John D French wrote the letter.
2 He is Director of the Office for National Data Collection.
3 His office is at Government Buildings, Bristol Road, Newport, Gwent.
4 The letter is addressed to Fidgets Ltd.
5 14 Rust Avenue, Luton, Bedfordshire.

Thinking about it
1 (open answer)   2 (open answer)
3 Its main purpose is to ask the company to provide some information for a survey, and to let them know that someone will be contacting them shortly to discuss things further.
4 It is an element of the Government's National Accounts on which economic policies are based.
5 If the forms are completed no further forms for any business survey run by that office will be sent for the next three years.
6 (open answer)
7 A member of their staff will be contacting Fidgets Ltd.

Thinking it through
1 (open answer)
2 He ends the letter in this way because he does not know the name of the person he is writing to. (If he did know the name, the letter would be signed 'Yours sincerely'.) He includes his title so the reader knows what job he does.
3 (open answer)
4 (open answer)

⇨ *Copymaster* **Official Language**
Three different examples of official language in texts are provided here for study and discussion.

Official Language

Name _____ Date _____

This extract comes from a typical motor insurance policy.

We shall not be liable in respect of any accident, injury, loss or damage occurring while any motor car insured by this policy is being
a) used for any purpose not permitted by the effective Certificate of Motor Insurance
b) driven by any person not described in the effective Certificate of Motor Insurance as a person entitled to drive
c) driven by you unless you hold a licence to drive such a motor car or have held and are not disqualified for holding or obtaining such a licence
d) driven with your permission by any person who to your knowledge does not hold a licence to drive such a motor car unless such person has held and is not disqualified for holding or obtaining such a licence.
While your car is in the custody or control of a member of the motor trade and used only for the purpose of its service upkeep or repair the indemnity provided to you is not affected by exceptions a) and b) above.

These are the conditions which apply to the use of a money-saving voucher for a chain of restaurants.

Conditions of use:
1 Voucher entitles the bearer to £3 off the restaurant bill for every £15 spent.
2 Voucher valid all day Monday to Friday and Saturday until 3 pm until 10 December.
3 Voucher valid against purchase of food and drink, and must be presented at the time of ordering.
4 Voucher cannot be exchanged for cash or used in conjunction with any other offer.

This is part of an author's contract with a publisher.

Acceptance of Work

The Publishers shall accept the Work provided that the complete typescript as delivered by the Author conforms to a reasonable extent in nature, scope and style to the specifications set out in Schedule A of this Agreement: and they shall have the right as a condition of acceptance of the Work to require amendments by the Author to ensure the Work does so conform. If the Author is unable or unwilling to undertake such amendments or arrange for them to be made within such reasonable period of time as shall have been agreed by the Publishers, then the Publishers shall, after consultation with the Author, have the right to employ a competent person or persons to make the amendments and any fees payable shall be deducted from any sums due to the Author under the terms of this Agreement.

Focus on Comprehension Teacher's Book 'C' Text © Louis Fidge 1999 Illustrations © Nelson 1999 Published by Thomas Nelson and Sons Ltd

FURTHER TEACHING OPPORTUNITIES

Text level

Reading comprehension
▶ Explain that the play was written a long time ago and contains some old-fashioned language. Talk briefly about the importance of William Shakespeare to our literary heritage. Read the whole play script once right the way through with the group or class without explanation to give children the gist. Ask them to summarise the passage in their own words.
▶ Identify and discuss some of the conventions of the layout of play scripts: character parts, scene setting, instructions to the actors. How are these set out in the text?
▶ Spend some time studying and trying to interpret the language of the play.

Writing composition
▶ Ask children to write an act of a modern version of a shipwreck, loosely based on the text in the unit, in the form of a play.

Sentence level

Grammatical awareness
▶ Ask children to adapt the text and rewrite it in a simpler form, in modern English.

Sentence construction and punctuation
▶ Punctuation marks give important signals to actors on how to say their lines. Study the use of the many different types of punctuation mark in the play, and discuss their functions.

Word level

Spelling
▶ Find examples of words containing the following common word endings in the play: 'ore', 'al', 'or', 'er', 'ure', 'ance', 'ent' 'ant', 'age', 'ace', 'sion'. Ask children to supply at least two more words containing each letter pattern.

Vocabulary extension
▶ Find words in the text that can have two meanings: for example, page, present, address. Ask children to write pairs of sentences using the words in different ways, which make their meanings clear.

ANSWERS

Thinking back
1 a shipwreck; 2 Illyria; 3 Elysium; 4 the Governor of Illyria; 5 pages; 6 as a man; 7 Olivia; 8 mansion.

Thinking about it
1 Yes. There were 'some half dozen survivors'.
2 (open answer)
3 She was travelling with her brother and is worried he may have been drowned.
4 (open answer)
5 (open answer)
6 The lines that tell you are: Cesario, thou knowest no less but all: I have unclasped to thee the book even of my secret soul.
7 Viola gazes at him, and it is evident that her feelings towards him are somewhat stronger than those of a page for his master. Yet ... who'er I woo, I myself would be his wife!
8 He sends Cesario to tell her the Duke loves her.

Thinking it through
1 (open answer)   2 (open answer)
3 a) What do you sailors think?
  b) He has only known you for three days.
  c) I have told you all of my most private secrets.
  d) Go and see her.
  e) Make sure she lets you in.
4 The words that might be spoken by a narrator.
5 William Shakespeare wrote the original version.
6 (open answer)

▷ *Copymaster* **Ancient and Modern**
This amusing poem is in two parts and is ideal for performing. One part is in medieval English, the other in modern English.

Name _____   Date _____

Enjoy reading this dramatic poem.
Write a suitable ending for it, in the same style.

Once upon a time
　　Last week
In a dark dank castle yard
　　our playground
Stood a modest misty-eyed maiden
　　our Vicky
In the grip of a scaly spotted serpent
　　Wayne Smith

And its oily orc-like allies
　　Ian and Alan
The valiant virile warrior
　　me
Strode through the mighty portal
　　the school gates
Bearing his sharp and shiny sword and dagger
　　compass and ruler
And roaring, 'Avaunt ye miscreants and malefactors!'
　　Oi you!
'Unhand yon pure and matchless maid upon the instant!'
　　Geroff our Vicky
There ensued a bloody bruising battle
　　a big scrap
Which will be remembered in the great tales of heroic deeds:
　　till next week
But then the clamorous din diminished
　　it went quiet
And they cowered in the shadow of an even mightier and more menacing monster
　　the Head
Whose nostrils breathed forth fire and eyes flashed most fearsome
　　he was not pleased

Trevor Millum

Focus on Comprehension Teacher's Book 'C'　Text © Louis Fidge 1999 Illustrations © Nelson 1999　Published by Thomas Nelson and Sons Ltd

FURTHER TEACHING OPPORTUNITIES

Text level

Reading comprehension

▶ Ask children what Amanda's usual response to her Mum's nagging is. Is the poem a one-way or two-way conversation? Discuss how Amanda's responses to her Mum could be considered as escapism.

▶ Contrast the everyday, practical concerns of the mother with the vivid figurative images being imagined by Amanda.

▶ Consider how it is clear from the layout who is saying what.

▶ Point out that not all the verses rhyme. (Only Amanda's do.)

Writing composition

▶ Ask children to rewrite the poem as a play script.

▶ Ask children to write a similar poem, based on their own experiences of being nagged, and substituting their own dreams and thoughts in place of Amanda's.

Sentence level

Grammatical awareness

▶ Notice the imperative nature of many of the mother's commands. Which are couched as negatives? Which are statements with a negative implication?

Sentence construction and punctuation

▶ Ask children to make up some things Amanda might have dreamed, using conditionals like 'if … then …', 'I might have …', 'If I could …', 'I would …'.

Word level

Spelling

▶ Find the word 'languid' in the poem. Ask children to use a dictionary to find words beginning with 'gu' and followed by another vowel. List ten.

Vocabulary extension

▶ Point out how the word 'freedom' is changed from an adjective into a noun by the addition of a suffix. List a range of common adjectives and supply a number of common suffixes, such as 'dom', 'tion', 'ness', 'ment', 'ance', 'ery', 'ure'. Encourage children to make up their own 'new' nouns, such as closedom, hungriance.

ANSWERS

Thinking back

1 your nails; 2 that chocolate; 3 slouching; 4 your shoulders; 5 your acne; 6 look at me when I'm speaking to you; 7 you to clean your shoes; 8 your homework?; 9 I nagged you; 10 your room?

Thinking about it

1 (open answer) She probably does not do as she is told. Her Mum is always nagging her.

2 Amanda bites her nails. She hunches her shoulders and slouches. Amanda is not good at doing her homework. She has an untidy room. She does not clean her shoes often. Amanda has acne. She sulks when told off, and she is moody.

3 (open answer)

4 (open answer)

5 (open answer)

Thinking it through

1 What Mum is saying is in normal print. Amanda's words are in italics.

2 (open answer)   3 (open answer)

4 Yes, because Amanda's thoughts are all imaginary.

⇨ *Copymaster*
Mary and Sarah

Amanda and her Mum had very differing points of view – and so do Mary and Sarah. This poem makes a good contrast with that in the unit, and may be read in two parts. Excellent for work on antonyms!

Mary and Sarah

Name _____   *Date* _____

Mary likes smooth things
Things that glide:
Sleek skis swishing down a mountainside.

Sarah likes rough things,
Things that snatch:
Boats with barnacled bottoms, thatch.

Mary likes smooth things,
Things all mellow:
Milk, silk, runny honey, tunes on a cello.

Sarah likes rough things,
Things all troubly:
Crags, snags, bristles, thistles, fields left stubbly.

Mary says – polish,
Sarah says – rust,
Mary says – mayonnaise,
Sarah says – crust.

Sarah says – hedgehogs,
Mary says – seals,
Sarah says – sticklebacks,
Mary says – eels.

Give me, says Mary,
The slide of a stream,
The touch of a petal,
A bowl of ice cream.

Give me, says Sarah,
The gales of a coast,
The husk of a chestnut,
A plate of burnt toast.

Mary and Sarah –
They'll never agree
Till peaches and coconuts
Grow on one tree.

From *A Mouse in my Roof* by Richard Edwards

Focus on Comprehension Teacher's Book 'C'   Illustrations © Nelson 1999   Published by Thomas Nelson and Sons Ltd

FURTHER TEACHING OPPORTUNITIES

Text level

Reading comprehension

▶ Study the words of each verse and help children recognise the poet's effective use of descriptive language.

▶ Ask children to articulate personal responses to the poem, identifying how and why it affects them.

▶ Encourage children to articulate what they notice about the structure and form of the poem. Get them to count and note the syllable patterns of the lines. Explain what a haiku is (a Japanese poetry form which consists of three lines containing seventeen syllables in all: 5, 7, 5).

Writing composition

▶ (Refer to the copymaster.)

Sentence level

Grammatical awareness

▶ Use the poem as a basis for reviewing work on word classes (parts of speech). Select one particular class of word at a time, say nouns. Read through the poem and identify all the nouns. Ask children to say whether each noun is singular or plural. Apply the same sort of approach to other classes of words: verbs, adjectives, adverbs, pronouns, prepositions, and so on.

Sentence construction and punctuation

▶ Taking notice of punctuation when reading poetry is essential to gain proper understanding. Read this poem several times. paying special attention to the punctuation marks.

Word level

Spelling

▶ Use the following nouns from the text: 'branch', 'ear', 'baby'. Ask children to write them in the plural. Ask children to note what happens. Provide them with a variety of other words that fall into these categories to pluralise:
  – regular words that just take 's';

  – words ending in 'sh' (dish), 'ch' (stitch), 'x' (fox) that take 'es';
  – words ending in a consonant + 'y' (lady, fairy) in which the 'y' is changed to 'i' and 'es' is added.
  Ask children to make up rules to cover how each set of words is pluralised.
  What happens to words that end in 'f' or 'fe' (shelf, wife), or 'o' (potato)?

Vocabulary extension

▶ Ask children to write a definition of their own for each animal and then to place the animal definitions in alphabetical order. Check their definitions against those in a dictionary and discuss any major differences.

ANSWERS

Thinking back

1 Ten animals; 2 in a stable; 3 angels singing; 4 washing its feet; 5 safe; 6 kneeling; 7 decorating with an olive branch; 8 in the roof, above the baby.

Thinking about it

1 so they don't wake the baby.
2 by purring.
3 The owl has given up hunting.
4 The hills are bleak.
5 (open answer)
6 The spider's web sparkles like a star.
7 (open answer)
8 A stable is a place in which animals are kept. A manger is a trough for animal food.

Thinking it through

1 (open answer)   2 (open answer)
3 There are ten verses.
4 (open answer)
5 Line 1 = 5 syllables. Line 2 = 7 syllables. Line 3 = 5 syllables.

🔸 *Copymaster*   **Count the Syllables**
This copymaster contains a haiku, a cinquain and a tanka poem to compare and discuss.

Count the Syllables

Name _____   Date _____

Some poetic forms consist
of a controlled number of
syllables and lines.

A *haiku* has three lines
Line 1 has 5 syllables
Line 2 has 7 syllables
Line 3 has 5 syllables.

A *cinquain* has five lines.
Line 1 has 2 syllables
Line 2 has 4 syllables
Line 3 has 6 syllables
Line 4 has 8 syllables
Line 5 has 2 syllables.

A *tanka* has five lines.
Line 1 has 5 syllables
Line 2 has 7 syllables
Line 3 has 5 syllables
Line 4 has 7 syllables
Line 5 has 7 syllables.

**Count the syllables and lines. Write what
sort of poem each of the following is.**

Swaying in the wind
As the breeze slips through my leaves,
I start to shiver.
Nobody looks up at me.
I think nobody likes me.

_____

I saw
Six silly snails
Sliding on dustbin lids
They slipped and slithered and fell off.
Crick! Crack!

_____

A tongue-dangling dog
Lollops languidly along
In the hot sunshine.

_____

Choose one of these types of poems.
Try writing one yourself.

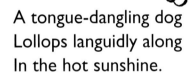

Do it in rough on another sheet
of paper first. Write your finished
copy on this sheet.

Focus on Comprehension Teacher's Book 'C'   Text © Louis Fidge 1999 Illustrations © Nelson 1999   Published by Thomas Nelson and Sons Ltd

FURTHER TEACHING OPPORTUNITIES

Text level

Reading comprehension

▶ Note the fact that this is from a book by Charles Dickens. Ask children for anything they know about him. Explain that he is a famous author from the Victorian period, that his books are still read frequently today, and that many have been made into films or adapted for TV, such as Oliver Twist, Great Expectations. Ask children to look out for examples of things or words that give clues to the period, and take the opportunity to discuss expressions or unusual vocabulary.

▶ Where is the passage set? Discuss what we can learn of the household and people in it.

▶ Ask children to find words and phrases in the text that convey happiness and excitement. Ask children to suggest reasons why 'classics' such as this have such enduring appeal.

Writing composition

▶ Ask children to write about their opinions of the passage – what did they enjoy (or not like) about it?

▶ Get children to use information in the text, and their imaginations, to write a description of how they imagine the rest of the day was spent.

Sentence level

Grammatical awareness

▶ Find and list examples of verbs and adjectives in the passage. Discuss their effectiveness. Try replacing them with other synonyms. Try leaving them out. Notice and discuss what effect this has on meaning.

Sentence construction and punctuation

▶ The passage contains a lot of reported speech. Ask children to record some of the dialogue as direct speech and note the differences.

▶ Encourage the children to make a very brief summary of the text in a given number of words, say 100.

Word level

Spelling

▶ Have a word hunt competition. See who can come up with the most examples of words containing each of these letter patterns in the text: 'ble', 'au', 'air', 'ie', 'ear', 'oar', 'our', 'ight', 'ough', 'ous,' 'ei'.

Vocabulary extension

▶ Encourage children to rewrite some of the paragraphs in simpler modern language, yet retaining the spirit of the text. Compare and contrast different versions.

▶ Find and list words from the text that we do not use much these days.

ANSWERS

Thinking back
1 True   2 False   3 Can't tell   4 False   5 True

Thinking about it
1 Mrs Cratchit, Bob Cratchit, Master Peter, Miss Belinda, Martha, Tiny Tim were all at the Christmas Dinner.
2 (open answer) There was a murmur of delight probably because the goose looked so nice, especially when Mrs Cratchit cut it and the stuffing came out.
3 'Everyone had had enough and the youngest Cratchits in particular, were steeped in sage-and-onion to the eyebrows!'
4 He said the pudding was wonderful. He said it was the greatest success achieved by Mrs Cratchit since their marriage.
5 (open answer)

Thinking it through
1 (open answer)   2 (open answer)
3 (open answer)   4 (open answer)
5 a) The passage came from A Christmas Carol.
   b) It was written by Charles Dickens.
   c) (open answer)

⇨ *Copymaster*   **People and Places**
Two more Dickens' extracts are provided (from *Oliver Twist* and *Nicholas Nickleby*) for comparison with the one in the unit.

People and Places

Name _____   Date _____

Read these extracts from books by Charles Dickens.
Compare them with each other, and with the extract
in Unit 15, for style and use of language.

A description of the Artful Dodger
(from *Oliver Twist*)

He was snub-nosed, flat-browed,
common-faced boy enough; and as
dirty a juvenile as one would wish to
see; but he had about him the airs
and manners of a man. He was short
for his age; with rather bow-legs, and
little, sharp, ugly eyes. He wore a
man's coat which reached nearly to
his heels. He had turned the cuffs
back, half-way up his arm, to get his
hands out of the sleeves.

A description of Dotheboy's Hall
(from *Nicholas Nickleby*)

It was a bare and dirty room, with a couple
of windows, whereof a tenth part might be
glass, the remainder being stopped up with
copybooks and paper. There were a couple
of long, old rickety desks, cut and notched,
and inked, and damaged in every possible
way; two or three forms, a detached desk for
Mr Squeers, and another for his assistant.
The ceiling was supported, like that of a
barn, by cross beams and rafters; and the
walls were so stained and discoloured that it
was impossible to tell whether they had ever
been touched with paint or whitewash.

Focus on Comprehension Teacher's Book 'C'   Text © Louis Fidge 1999 Illustrations © Nelson 1999   Published by Thomas Nelson and Sons Ltd

FURTHER TEACHING OPPORTUNITIES

Text level

Reading comprehension
▶ Make the point that it is important to listen to arguments from all angles, before making up your mind on issues. Read the article in the newspaper. What facts does it contain? Which are personal opinions? How 'reasonable' does it sound? Next read each set of arguments one at a time. Discuss the merits and shortcomings of each set of views.
▶ Ask children to identify any powerfully emotive words used on the posters. Discuss some of the strategies the protesters used. Which do the children think might be most effective?

Writing composition
▶ (Refer to the copymaster.)

Sentence level

Grammatical awareness
▶ Find examples of, and discuss, the following different features in the text: a fairly formal, impersonal style of writing; the presentation of facts; the expression of personal opinions; the use of persuasive language; the use of the present and future tenses; the use of conditionals; the use of the third person; the use of 'official' language and terms.

Sentence construction and punctuation
▶ Ask the children to summarise in note form the arguments for and against the development.

Word level

Spelling
▶ Select a good number of words from the letters that have been transformed in some way, say by prefixing or suffixing. Ask the children to identify the root word from which each is derived and what changes have been made. Discuss if the transformation has affected the spelling of the root word in any way. Discuss what type of word the root word is and what type

of word it became after transformation (if it changed its word class in any way): for example, scavengers (noun, plural) becomes scavenge (verb).

Vocabulary extension
▶ Many people write to an MP about issues. MP is an abbreviation. Ask children to suggest other common acronyms or abbreviations. Consider what they stand for.

ANSWERS

Thinking back
1 Fordham Common is a large area of open land on the outskirts of Fordham.
2 It is used for things like sport and leisure (walking the dog, playing football).
3 There are plans to build a biscuit factory there.
4 Many people read about the plans in the newspaper (*The Fordham Times*).
5 It will mean there will be nowhere to play sport or to go for walks. It will bring more traffic to the area. It will bring more pollution.
6 It will bring new jobs. It will bring trade to the local shops. It will bring more life into the local area.

Thinking about it
1 (open answer)   2 (open answer)
3 (open answer)   4 (open answer)
5 (open answer)

Thinking it through
1 (open answer)   2 (open answer)
3 (open answer)   4 (open answer)

⇨▶ *Copymaster*
Advantages and Disadvantages
Children are asked to consider the advantages and disadvantages of being tall and small, and to decide which of the options is best.

Advantages and Disadvantages

Name _____   *Date* _____

**Write down the advantages and disadvantages
of being tall and those of being small.**

Being tall		Being small	
Advantages	Disadvantages	Advantages	Disadvantages

Choose which you believe is best. Write a persuasive argument in favour of your view, but also take into account the other side of the argument.

I would rather be _____ because I think _____

_____

_____

_____

_____

However some people think that it is better to be _____ but I do not

agree because _____

_____

_____

_____

Focus on Comprehension Teacher's Book 'C'   Text © Louis Fidge 1999 Illustrations © Nelson 1999   Published by Thomas Nelson and Sons Ltd

FURTHER TEACHING OPPORTUNITIES

Text level

▶ Ask children to comment critically on the impact and effectiveness of the poem. What was its theme? How does the poet make the reader think of pollution as evil? Is the linkage between dragons and pollution a helpful image?

▶ Ask children how the poet develops the theme and structures the poem.

▶ Ask children in what sense most of the dragons mentioned are 'visible' but the last dragon is 'invisible'?

Writing composition

▶ Ask children to write a review of the poem, considering its theme, structure, style and effectiveness, as well as personal responses to it.

▶ Ask the children to compare this poem with 'How Can You Buy the Sky' in Unit 2. Which do they prefer? How are the themes similar? Which is more effective? How similar are the styles and structures of both poems? Are they both 'modern' poems?

Sentence level

Grammatical awareness

▶ Ask children to summarise the main theme of each verse in one sentence, using the passive form of the verb: for example, the air is filled with lead by the dragon in the motor car.

Sentence construction and punctuation

▶ Use the poem as an opportunity to revise the use of apostrophes for contractions and possession.

Word level

Spelling

▶ Write out the pairs of rhyming words from the poem. Which contain the same letter patterns? Which rhyme but have different letter patterns? Ask children to try to think of other rhyming words that a) have the same letter pattern, b) have a different letter pattern for each word.

▶ Use the word 'invisible' to focus on the use of prefixes and the way they change the meaning of words. Extend this to further work on prefixes such as 'sub', 'bi', 'tri', 'con', 'ex'. Use the dictionary to find more words with these prefixes.

▶ 'Saliva' is interesting because it ends in 'a'. Brainstorm other words that end in a consonant + vowel (other than 'e').

Vocabulary extension

▶ Ask children to experiment with creating similes and metaphors related to the theme: for example, car exhaust fumes are evil spirits which creep up and choke you.

ANSWERS

1 lead; 2 smoke; 3 oil; 4 fish; 5 crops and grass; 6 wreaths

Thinking about it

1 The 'dragon' in the car is petrol and diesel oil.
2 (open answer)   3 (open answer)
4 (open answer)
5 a) noxious: harmful to living things
   b) wreath: a garland of flowers or leaves often used at funerals.
6 (open answer)

Thinking it through

1 The dragons are bad, because they refer to things that pollute the environment. This poem is really about pollution.
2 (open answer)   3 (open answer)

⇨ *Copymaster* **Using Imagination**
In the poem in the unit, pollution is likened to a dragon. The selection of poems on this copymaster involve the use of a variety of vivid images also, for comparison and discussion.

⇨➤ Using Imagination

In Unit 17, pollution is likened to a dragon.
These poems involve the use of vivid images also.

In his sleep my poodle
Is a Doberman,
Black, shiny-coated and tough.
No-one picks on him.
When he smiles, his sharp white teeth glint wickedly.
In his dreams.

In the cupboard
Below the stairs
There lurks an evil octopus,
With curled up tentacles,
Waiting to slip its slithery arms around me
And drag me into the dark lair.
Below the stairs.

The headlights of the car
Are two luminous monster's eyes,
That dazzle and blind in the night
As they swish by.

The sound of the wind at night –
A howling werewolf on a hill,
A thousand snakes hissing,
The moaning drone of an angry swarm of bees.

Thick fog on the road –
The creeping fingers of the mysterious monster of the mist,
The folds of an old man's beard,
Cushions of clouds.

An old leafless tree –
Brittle remains of a long-extinct dinosaur,
A cry of pain,
Death.

FURTHER TEACHING OPPORTUNITIES

Text level

Reading comprehension

▶ After reading the text, ask children to write a character profile for Howard, Joe and Miss Tate, from information explicitly stated and inferred.

▶ Discuss how Miss Tate is portrayed as a stereotypical teacher.

▶ Ask children to suggest reasons why Joe had a very low self-esteem.

Writing composition

▶ Ask children to write a book blurb for the back cover of the book from which the extract is taken, based on the text in the unit. Give children 100 words in which to do it.

Sentence level

Grammatical awareness

▶ The story is written in the first person. Experiment by rewriting sections of it in the third person and considering what changes are required.

Sentence construction and punctuation

▶ Study selected sentences from the passage. Work out how many clauses each sentence contains. Note where connectives or conjunctions are used to join them together. Discuss which is the main clause in each sentence. Experiment with sentences structures by moving clauses about within complex sentences and seeing what difference this makes to meaning, and what changes are required to the wording.

Word level

Spelling

▶ Use the verbs 'peer', 'try', 'admit' and 'warble' from the text. Try writing each in the present tense by adding 's' and 'ing' and in the past tense by adding 'ed'. Note what happens (if anything) to the spelling of the root word when the suffixes are added. Ask children to think of other examples of verbs which fit the same patterns. Make up a rule for each set of verbs.

▶ Find examples of irregular past tenses of verbs (those which don't end in 'ed', such as 'sunk') in the text and record these. Ask children to write the root verb from which each comes.

Vocabulary extension

▶ Ask children to select a number of more difficult words from the text and to invent riddles, word searches or crosswords including them.

ANSWERS

1 Howard.
2 Joe Gardener.
3 Miss Tate.
4 tidy his desk.
5 He asked Howard if the thing was trash (rubbish to be thrown away) or treasure (important things to be kept).
6 a pound, a dental appointment card, Howard's special sheet of paper with words on it to help Howard with his spelling.
7 spelling and writing.
8 making models.

Thinking about it

1 You can tell Howard is new by the fact that Miss Tate had to explain the class rules to him.
2 a) (open answer)   b) (open answer)
3 (open answer)
4 a) Howard is new to the school. He is sorry for Joe. He doesn't have a high regard for teachers.
b) Joe is a poor speller. His writing is not very good. His desk is in a mess.
c) Miss Tate is a teacher. Her desk is at the front of the class. She is rather fussy.

Thinking it through

1 (open answer)   2 (open answer)
3 (open answer)   4 (open answer)
5 (open answer)   6 (open answer)

➡ *Copymaster* **Reading and Feelings**
This copymaster encourages children to empathise with situations in the unit.

Reading and Feelings

Name _____ *Date* _____

Think of how you felt at different places in the story 'Trash or Treasure'. Write about five different feelings you had.

I felt _____ when _____

_____

_____

I felt _____ when _____

_____

_____

I felt _____ when _____

_____

_____

I felt _____ when _____

_____

_____

I felt _____ when _____

_____

_____

Book 4 / Copymaster / Unit 18

Focus on Comprehension Teacher's Book 'C'   Text © Louis Fidge 1999 Illustrations © Nelson 1999   Published by Thomas Nelson and Sons Ltd

FURTHER TEACHING OPPORTUNITIES

Text level

Reading comprehension

▶ Before reading the text, ask children to have a quick look at the passage as a whole, at the illustrations and then read the introductory 'Think ahead' section. Ask children what the theme of the text is going to be. Ask them to volunteer any knowledge they may have on the subject and to raise questions they would like to see answered in the text.

▶ Close-read the text right the way through. Follow this by specific questions related to the factual content of the text, requiring children to scan for the specific answers.

▶ Ask children which of the sections they find most interesting and why.

▶ Ask children for their opinion on the structure, presentation and layout. Was it easy to find their way around? How clearly structured was it? What 'signposts' are there to help the reader?

Writing composition

▶ Use the text as an opportunity for developing note-taking skills.

Sentence level

Grammatical awareness

▶ Find examples of the following features of information texts: fairly formal style of writing; the presentation of facts; the use of the present tense; the use of technical language and terms.

Sentence construction and punctuation

▶ There are several examples of more sophisticated punctuation marks in the text such as inverted commas, hyphens, dashes, brackets. Discuss their functions. Find and discuss as many different uses for commas as possible in the text.

Word level

Spelling

▶ Identify and list polysyllabic words from the text. Say them and work out how many syllables each consists of. Mark in syllable boundaries in the words. Consider which of the syllables are stressed and unstressed in the words.

Vocabulary extension

▶ Ask the children to choose some difficult words from the text. Find and write the definitions for them, and give the definitions only to a partner to match with the correct words in the text.

ANSWERS

Thinking back

1 To allow our bodies to rest and recover from the rigours of the day.
2 We can become tired, clumsy and sluggish the following day, and find it difficult to concentrate.
3 'Jet lag' is when our 'time clocks' have become mixed up because of passing through time zones in an aeroplane.
4 We need less sleep.
5 Eight hours' sleep a day.
6 a) Horses   b) Bats
7 Four stages.
8 We need it to refresh ourselves.
9 Rapid Eye Movement.
10 When we are dreaming.

Thinking about it

1 (open answer)   2 (open answer)
3 (open answer)
4 horses, rabbits and humans, cats, hamsters, squirrels, bats
5 a) rigours: hardships   b) sluggish: slow to move
   c) temporary: for a limited period of time
   d) transition: change from one state to another
   e) rapid: quick
6 Nap, doze, slumber.

Thinking it through

1 a) It is helpful because each section is about a different aspect of the topic.
   b) (open answer)
2 (open answer)   3 (open answer)

⇨ *Copymaster*
Working out the Meaning
Children are asked to work out the meanings of a variety of common expressions and idioms.

➡ Work out the Meaning

Name _____   Date _____

1 We cannot always take words at face value – they do not always mean exactly what they say. Match up these common expressions with their actual meanings:

having forty winks	to stop people having fun
let sleeping dogs lie	having a nap
to be a wet blanket	don't cause trouble, leave things as they are
to keep in the dark	to keep some important information from someone

2 Write the word or phrase from this box that means the same as the expression in bold in each sentence below.

everyone   main purpose   level   mad

At the finishing post the horses were **neck and neck**.   _____

His friends thought he was **round the bend**.   _____

Winning is not the **be-all and end-all** of sport.   _____

The football match was attended by **all and sundry**.   _____

3 Write the expression from this box that means the same as the words in bold in each sentence below.

in the long run   bite the dust   once in a blue moon   throw in the towel

I go to the cinema **on very rare occasions.**   _____

When he became bankrupt, the shopkeeper decided to **give up**.   _____

I expected to win but after being beaten I had to **admit failure**.   _____

I failed the test the first time but was sure I would succeed **eventually**.   _____

Focus on Comprehension Teacher's Book 'C'   Text © Louis Fidge 1999 Illustrations © Nelson 1999   Published by Thomas Nelson and Sons Ltd

FURTHER TEACHING OPPORTUNITIES

Text level

Reading comprehension

▶ After reading the passage ask for children's responses to it. How would they describe this type of story? Did they like it/dislike it? Were they enthralled by it?

▶ Study the opening two paragraphs. Ask children to comment critically on them as a) 'openers' for a story b) descriptions of a character.

▶ Focus on the author's style and vivid use of language.

Writing composition

▶ Ask children to write a report of the meeting that took place between Cluny and Redtooth, and the Abbot, Constance and Mathias.

Sentence level

Grammatical awareness

▶ Use the text to revise the use of adverbs.

Sentence construction and punctuation

▶ See Writing Composition above.

Word level

Spelling

▶ Ask children to find some tricky words from the text, such as masonry. Ask children for suggestions on how they might remember the spellings of these words.

Vocabulary extension

▶ Read through the text and list words to do with a) armour, b) weapons, c) the Abbey building. Ask children to define unfamiliar words by reference to the text and dictionaries.

ANSWERS

Thinking back

1 a rat.
2 the Scourge.
3 a ragged black cloak made of bat wings, fastened at the throat with a mole skull, and a war helmet with the plumes of a blackbird and the horns of a stag beetle.
4 one of Cluny's soldiers.
5 howls of derison and some loose pieces of masonry thrown from the ramparts.
6 Matthias said Redtooth and Cluny could enter.
7 Redtooth was worried.
8 Constance demanded that they throw it off.
9 Matthias was concerned about Cluny's tail because he used it as a weapon.
10 They carried staves.

Thinking about it

Cluny and his army approached Redwall Abbey.

Matthias said that Cluny and Redtooth could enter the Abbey without their army.

Constance demanded that Cluny and Redtooth took off their armour.

Matthias insisted that Cluny tie his tail around his waist.

The Abbey gates were opened to allow the two rats to enter.

Constance and Matthias met Cluny and Redtooth when they came in the Abbey.

The mice were unhappy to leave the Abbot unguarded.

Cluny leapt in the air and made the mice scatter in panic.

Thinking it through

1 (open answer)
2 a) (open answer)   b) (open answer)
  c) (open answer)   d) (open answer)
3 a) The Abbey had high, thick walls with parapets on top. It had a heavy gate in one wall.
  b) many woodland creatures (mice, badgers), sheltering from Cluny's army.
  c) (open answer)
4 a) walked in a jaunty fashion; b) looked through partly closed eyes; c) the part of a helmet covering the face; d) scornfully; e) walls built as a defence against an enemy; f) someone held captive as a guarantee that promises made by the enemy will be kept; g) a great number or crowd; h) a meeting of many people for a discussion

▷ *Copymaster* **Heroes and Villains**
Children are asked to compare the qualities of the characters of Cluny and Matthias.

Heroes and Villains

Name _____   Date _____

Compare the qualities of the hero Matthias (M)

and the villain Cluny (C).

**Think about what they did, said and how they behaved in Unit 20.
Colour in the block graph to show the percentage of their good
and bad qualities.**

		percentage										
		0	10	20	30	40	50	60	70	80	90	100
friendly	M											
	C											
honest	M											
	C											
brave	M											
	C											
thoughtful	M											
	C											
clever	M											
	C											
trustworthy	M											
	C											
caring	M											
	C											
fierce	M											
	C											
arrogant	M											
	C											
devious	M											
	C											
aggressive	M											
	C											
proud	M											
	C											

**Compare your results with others. Discuss any major differences.
Find examples to justify your views in the text.**

Focus on Comprehension Teacher's Book 'C'   Text © Louis Fidge 1999 Illustrations © Nelson 1999   Published by Thomas Nelson and Sons Ltd

FURTHER TEACHING OPPORTUNITIES

Text level

Reading comprehension

▶ Discuss the different reasons why people keep diaries. Read the diary extract a couple of times. Ask children for their immediate response to it.

▶ Select some sentences and ask children to suggest why they sound so strange to our ears today.

▶ Find some of the facts Crusoe states and some personal opinions he expresses.

Writing composition

▶ Discuss with the children other things that Crusoe might have seen and written about. Brainstorm ideas and note them down. Ask children to write up a diary entry for the event.

Sentence level

Grammatical awareness

▶ Crusoe's writing is not standard English as we know it today. Ask children to rewrite parts of the extract as we would do so today.

Sentence construction and punctuation

▶ The diary uses many connecting words and phrases, linking the account together, such as 'Toward night … and … which …'. Identify some of these and draw attention to how they are used to link together sequences of events.

Word level

Spelling

▶ List any words that are spelt differently from the way we spell them today. Write the modern spelling next to each.

▶ Ask the children to find words in the extract containing the common word endings 'able', 'ful', 'ant', 'ure', 'ise', 'ock', 'ible', 'ss', 'le', 'ar', 'age', 'ance', 'ent', 'tion'. Ask them to suggest and list other words ending in the same ways.

Vocabulary extension

▶ Ask the children to find some words which are not used much today. List them and ask children to write their own definitions for them.

ANSWERS

Thinking back

1 a) Daniel Defoe; b) Robinson Crusoe; c) a diary; d) People believed it was real because it was written so well and was so realistic.
2 He was shipwrecked.
3 1659 to 1660.
4 Two cats and the Captain's dog, Japp.
5 By cutting notches on a post.
6 Guns, gunpowder, pistol, sword, axe, saw, nails, ropes, blankets, clothes, sails, a hammock, biscuits, flour, rum, wine, a Bible, pen and ink and some compasses.
7 He covered the tent with long poles, and the poles with plants and leaves.

Thinking about it

1 He describes himself as 'poor, miserable …'.
2 He had no food, shelter, clothes, weapons or place to escape from wild animals. He was afraid of wild animals, starvation and being murdered.
3 (open answer)
4 He had a Bible to read.
5 (open answer)
6 So that he would be safer from attack.
7 Some earth crumbled down from the roof. Two posts cracked. The ground shook violently three times at about eight minute intervals. A great piece of rock fell down with a terrible noise. The sea became very rough. Then it rained.

Thinking it through

1 He also described his feelings and thoughts.
2 (open answer)
3 He often begins nouns with capital letters.
4 (open answer)
5 a) gloomy; b) ate; c) people who live on the island; d) got weaker; e) swinging bed of canvas, often hung between two trees; f) small v-shaped cut; g) astonished

▢▶ *Copymaster* **The Only Survivor**
Children are asked to imagine they are the only survivors in an aeroplane crash in the jungle.

The Only Survivor

Name _____   Date _____

Imagine you are travelling on an aeroplane and it crashes in dense jungle, miles away from anywhere. You are the only survivor. You cannot stay near the wreck. You cannot carry too much. You manage to rescue certain things from the aeroplane. Which ten things would you take with you? Give your reasons.

✓	Item	Reason for choosing it
	knife	
	magnifying glass	
	rope	
	blanket	
	flask of water	
	matches	
	spade	
	signal flare	
	torch	
	first aid kit	
	binoculars	
	magazine	
	milk powder	
	watch	
	compass	
	rucksack	

Now reduce your choice to five things. What will they be?

_____   _____   _____   _____   _____

Focus on Comprehension Teacher's Book 'C'   Text © Louis Fidge 1999   Illustrations © Nelson 1999   Published by Thomas Nelson and Sons Ltd

FURTHER TEACHING OPPORTUNITIES

Text level

Reading comprehension
- After reading the extract, ask children to map out, in note form, the main events of the story, identifying significant incidents and organising them in sequence. When finished, the notes should provide the 'bones' of the story.
- Select specific paragraphs, such as the paragraph beginning '"Very mysterious," said Mother.' Analyse how each paragraph is structured: for example, comments sequenced to follow the shifting thoughts of the character, examples listed to justify a point or reiterated to give it force.
- Ask children how the author has portrayed various characters, such as Gran, Will. Do they conform to a certain stereotype?

Writing composition
- Reread the last sentence of the extract. Ask children to use their imaginations and discuss and write how the story might develop. Encourage a variety of possibilities. As a starting point, write down their suggested ideas, phrases, words on the board. (Incidentally, 'My Friend Walter' turns out to be the great Tudor explorer and sailor Walter Raleigh. If appropriate, mention this. It might well stimulate an entirely new train of thinking!)

Sentence level

Grammatical awareness
- Point out that, when we speak, we often use abbreviated sentences, and non-standard English. Ask children to rewrite some of the dialogue as proper sentences in standard English.

Sentence construction and punctuation
- There are many examples of conditionals: for example, using words like 'might' 'would', 'could', speculating on possible causes, options and possibilities. Find and discuss some of these.

Word level

Spelling
- Select examples of words that have been suffixed in some way. Ask children to identify the root word in each and what part of speech it is. How has the spelling of the root word been changed by the addition of the suffix? How has its meaning been changed?

Vocabulary extension
- In the story Gran says, 'Nothing ventured, nothing gained.' Ask children what this means. Provide children with a range of other common idioms or sayings and ask them what they mean: for example, every cloud has a silver lining; to strike while the iron's hot; to smell a rat; to get into hot water.

ANSWERS

Thinking back
1 The Tower of London
2 reunion
3 writing
4 Bess
5 Aunt Ellie

Thinking about it
1 You can tell Father is surprised because he says 'Well I'm blowed!'.
2 You can tell Little Jimmy got excited because he waved his arms up and down in the air.
3 (open answer)   4 (open answer)
5 Mother told Will to be quiet because he was describing events in a blood-thirsty way.

Thinking it through
1 Bess is telling the story. We know because Mother addresses the story-teller as Bess.
2 (open answer)   3 (open answer)
4 (open answer)   5 (open answer)
6 (open answer)

⇨ *Copymaster* **History Detective**
A picture of Sir Walter Raleigh is provided, containing several incongruous things which were invented or discovered in modern times. Children have to identify these.

⇨ **History Detective**

Sir Walter Raleigh lived in the seventeenth century.
There are ten things in the picture he would never have seen. List them.

_____

_____

Write ten words which have recently entered our language (for example, trainers, wheelie). (You are not allowed any of the things in the picture!)

_____

_____

Why are new words needed?

_____

_____

Why do some words die out?

_____

_____

Focus on Comprehension Teacher's Book 'C'   Text © Louis Fidge 1999 Illustrations © Nelson 1999   Published by Thomas Nelson and Sons Ltd